Artisan
Stroud

CLARE HONEYFIELD

Artisan Stroud

CLARE HONEYFIELD

The
History
Press

Front cover image: Courtesy of Milligan Beaumont

First published 2021

The History Press
97 St George's Place
Cheltenham, Gloucestershire, GL50 3QB
www.thehistorypress.co.uk

British Library Cataloguing in Publication Data.
A catalogue record for this book is available from the British Library.

ISBN 978 0 7509 9322 7

Design by Jemma Cox
Printed in Europe by Imak Ltd

Contents

Foreword

Stroud is a constantly evolving community set in a rural location that has seen remarkable changes in a very short space of time. I moved here as student in 1972 when I lived in a tiny hamlet called Paradise, near Painswick. The Stroud I remember, despite its appearance as a cultural desert and a bit of a backwater, was inhabited by a long tradition of craftsmen and artists very much inspired by William Morris's belief in the revival of the Arts and Crafts Movement. Originally an area of light engineering, small businesses have thrived in replacing the rich tradition of the textiles industry, and the original industrial architecture is evident everywhere.

In 1972, the artists and crafts people were almost invisible in the area with a few exceptions, such as the Gloucestershire Guild of Craftsmen. When I first came to the area, I didn't realise I had moved to a rural backwater rich with cultural diversity and alternative lifestyle, but I was proud to be a 'hippie' and student of my time, at a moment when it was a rare thing to see young, long-haired, 'alternative-types'.

I became friends with Diana Lodge, an elderly artist who lived in the Slad Valley. Diana was one of the original Bohemians living in Chelsea, where she had been a life model for Eric Gill and his social circle. She moved to Slad where she painted beautiful, brilliantly coloured watercolours. Diana was an important role model and influence in my life, taking me under her wing. She was very gregarious and introduced me to lots of her friends, and held an annual Christmas party at her home in the Slad Valley where I met many Stroud artists.

I lived in Paradise for a little more than a year while I was a student at Cheltenham School of Art, and lived in many different places after I left, notably Cornwall, Stoke-on-Trent and California before returning to the Stroud valleys – I've always returned to the area as I have found it to be a very unusually warm and convivial place.

When I moved back, I bought Bethesda Chapel, a beautiful but derelict Baptist chapel in the village of Uley. I lived in the old school room at the back and curtained off an area for a studio while I gutted the building. I became very integrated in the life of the village and the chapel became a popular place for the children to come and hang out. They were interested to see my lifestyle in this glorious muddle of a building and were intrigued to see my work and have a go themselves.

In 1977, I lived in India for nine months and discovered a holy man in the south called Satya Sai Baba. When I returned to Uley, I was inspired by Baba's teaching about service. A short while later the idea of Prema Arts came to me one night and hit me on the head. I didn't even know what an arts centre was but had a vision for something I wanted to create. I was incredibly naïve and unworldly. Everybody said it was an impossible and crazy idea but it's still there today, thirty-five years later. This was a personal journey inspired by Baba's teachings.

The Sunday Times recently nominated Stroud as the best place to live in the UK – there is no doubt that the atmosphere of the town is irresistible. It is very friendly and accessible, and a great place to raise children and to 'start a new life in the country'. Many musicians and people working in the media have gravitated here; there is an abundance of festivals growing out of every part of the community; there are courses and workshops covering every interest you can imagine and many that you can't. There is a growing reputation for a food culture with more restaurants and coffee shops than you can count, and the Saturday farmers' market has a reputation that attracts visitors from far and wide. Stroud is colourful and very ecologically minded – being the home of Stop Ecocide and Ecotricity, and the first vegan football club, Forest Green Rovers.

The influx of young artists and their families has been a formative influence on Stroud. In addition to visual artists there is a much wider artistic community that includes theatre, literature, film and music. A wonderful variety of music is played in the town, including jazz, hip-hop, choirs and singing groups.

Andrew Wood, 2021

Andrew is an artist, sculptor and the founder of Prema Arts Centre in Uley. He lives and works in central Stroud where he practises his art daily and is the creator of 'The Word' in London Road.

About the Author

Clare Honeyfield first began working with creatives in 1990 when she started her first series of Made in Stroud makers' markets in a church hall in town. Somehow, she is not sure how, she and a friend ran a vegan café at the events, something that was rather ahead of its time. She also arranged puppet shows, a busker and a kids' corner as her three children were all under school age at the time.

The event moved to the Subscription Rooms Ballroom, where it caught the eye of Detmar and Isabella Blow through Clare's friend, Amery Blow. Over the following years, Clare tried to get funding for a directory of local makers, and Clare and Isabella tried to get planning permission to start an arts barn at Edge Farm, both without success.

After spending a year travelling around Europe and busking at markets in Tuscany and southern Spain, Clare returned and was aware of a community planning conference that had been organised by Stroud District Council. At this event, one of the most asked for things in the area was the revival of 'Made in Stroud'.

Funding became available and small projects started popping up. Clare approached the leisure and tourism officer with her cuttings book, explaining that she had started Made in Stroud and it had always been about community action rather than about writing reports.

The sum of £10,000, which had been earmarked for a feasibility study, was redirected to Clare to run a trial series of markets at the Cornhill. The officer said, 'I want you to include Food Links.' Clare replied, 'I don't like farmers, I'm a vegetarian.'

After some discussion, the market was planned to include farmers selling food that had been grown or reared to high standards as well as makers selling their crafts.

On 3 July 1999, Isabella Blow and Jasper Conran launched the first farmers' market – or Made in Stroud Market, as it was known at the time – for Clare, who had been hot desking and getting support for some months from the Stroud Valleys Project (SVP). (Isabella wore a Philip Treacy hat and an Alexander McQueen lilac lace dress with hemmed skirt.) At dinner after the launch event, Jasper Conran described Stroud as 'The Covent Garden of the Cotswolds' and suggested Clare should run a shop in town, saying, 'people shop every day'.

After six months of running a monthly event, the council agreed to allow the market to run twice monthly, and to continue funding regular cooking demos and entertainment from local buskers. Clare became a founding director of the National Association of Farmers' Markets and got involved in co-writing the criteria for food and drink stalls and land-based makers and the Safe Food Policy for farmers' markets in the UK, as well as becoming a regular speaker at the annual Farmers' Market Conference in the UK and visiting Californian farmers' markets.

Towards the end of 2000, Clare noticed an empty refurbished shop unit in Kendrick Street. She'd been asked by SVP to find her own premises and it had been suggested by makers for some years that she set up a shop, so she took the opportunity to meet the owner and discuss taking on the lease. The owner was looking for an ethical tenant who was working for the environment and the community, having had the building renovated to an eco-specification.

On 1 December 2000, the Made in Stroud shop was opened, with a farmers' market information point taking up half of the shop space. By this time, Clare was working with DEFRA, Gloucestershire County Council and the SEED Lottery Fund to set up local Food Links projects around the county as part of a group of facilitators and directors. Gloucestershire Food Links was instrumental in the decentralisation of procurement of ingredients for school dinners, introducing healthy local food projects to schools and linking farm visits, growing food and healthy eating with the curriculum and culture of school life.

Stroud Farmers' Market became the most awarded in the UK, and the most successful privately run farmers' market outside London, as well as one of the first weekly farmers' markets outside the city. It is largely cited as being one of the factors to contribute to Stroud's reincarnation from post-industrial down-at-heel town to being lauded by the national media as 'The best town to live in the UK'.

Since 2012, Clare has been sole director of the Made in Stroud shop and co-director of the Made in Stroud online shop. She has retrained as a yoga teacher and coach, and works with entrepreneurs and creatives, helping people to overcome blocks to success, something she still has to do herself on a daily basis.

Clare is interested in the common threads of success and the shared themes in the lives of successful people; the definition of success being that a person can live a life which is authentic to their values, making a living doing work that is their passion. She has volunteered as crew at Tony Robbins' Unleash the Power (UPW) course, helping to build the fire for the fire-walking challenge for 12,000 participants as part of 100-strong fire crew.

In her work as a coach, Clare finds that the most exciting thing is to witness people stepping into their power, realising they are good enough, and having the courage to follow their dreams and passions.

Recently, Clare has worked with the Gloucestershire Gateway Trust and Gloucester Services as a consultant to the buying team, encouraging more local makers and producers to strike up a working relationship with the farm shops at the award-winning services and to become suppliers.

Meanwhile, as COVID-19 struck, and in the absence of travel opportunities and gatherings, Clare has taken up year-round river swimming and running online coaching groups for women entrepreneurs and creatives. In November 2020, Clare was invited by coach Jean Pierre de Villiers to be a contributor to *Your Best Life*, a personal development book by twenty-two switched-on professionals, which was an immediate bestseller in multiple categories internationally.

Clare is a mum to four adult sons and a grandma to four small people. Her hobbies include trapeze, aerial hoop and aerial silks, and she is a keen advocate of healthy living and fitness as a route to increased vitality. Most of all, Clare is one of life's cheerleaders, and has surrounded herself with her own cheerleaders, something she says is 'essential for a successful life and totally attainable by anyone'.

Clare is available for one-to-one coaching, speaking engagements and collaborative projects.

Introduction

Do you have a favourite mug? A favourite jumper? A favourite ring? Can you put into words what it is you love about it? As a student of business studies in my teens, I became fascinated with the art college over the road. I would wander the corridors in my lunch breaks, studying the sketches on the noticeboards and the ceramics in the studios. I would regularly get asked by the tutors: 'Can I help you with anything?' 'No, thanks,' I'd say, 'just looking at the art.'

Around this time, I first visited Prema Arts in Uley with my mum. I can still clearly remember the bright colours of the textile exhibition by Bobbie Cox. I bought postcards of her work and put them up on my bedroom wall at home. Next to these I had a quote by E. F. Schumacher, the inside back cover of an Ecology Party leaflet: 'We must do what we conceive to be the right thing, and not bother our heads or burden our souls with whether we are going to be successful. Because if we don't do the right thing, we'll be doing the wrong thing, and we will just be a part of the disease and not a part of the cure.' That postcard wall still lives in my thinking.

I started working with artisans by accident really (necessity being the mother of all invention) when I was helping my husband at the time to market his handmade drums. From attending the very first Made in Stroud makers markets in 1990/1, I completely fell in love with the vibe of handmade work.

It is not just about the materials, skill, tradition and talent: it's about the people. How many times a year do we buy an item of clothing or an object for the house without knowing its origins? For all we know, it might have been made in a sweat shop by people who have no agency and who are not paid enough money to live. These could be people who work in dangerous or unpleasant conditions, and the chances are worryingly high. My hope is that this book, and the movement towards buying quality and shopping mindfully, will encourage us all in our purchasing decisions. If we were all just a little bit more conscious of how we shop, we could transform the way big corporations source products, which would lead to a massive positive impact globally on waste and consumption. Whether it is buying fair trade, organic cotton to support the cotton farmers in India or shopping local, we can all do our bit to create a better world.

Being enthusiastic about the aesthetic is about more than owning beautiful things: it is about what goes on behind the scenes, what sort of organisations we are supporting with our hard-earned cash, the culture we create with our purchases, our environmental impact and what all of this means for generations to come. This is true beauty.

Although Stroud may seem a small and, even insignificant, town, the net of our influence may spread wider than we imagine. Whilst travelling in northern California I visited a museum of traditional First Nation artefacts and costumes from all around the United States. I was astonished to see Stroud Scarlet, or 'trade cloth' as the fabric was known, incorporated into traditional tribal clothing and footwear from the length and breadth of the Continent. Red scraps wrapped, sewn and woven into history.

This book is a collection of stories – stories that live on in the fabric of the objects created by the makers. I hope you will learn a little more about how the pot on your table or the T-shirt you are wearing came into being. You will hear about the obstacles to success people have had to overcome, the traditions they draw upon and, more than that, you will hear their passion for their craft and the years of trial and error, training, studying and learning that have all gone into one beautiful object.

We are truly blessed to be surrounded by such a rich culture of making by hand. Maybe we could adopt 7th-generation thinking like the first nation American Haudenosaunee people, who lived by the philosophy that 'the decisions made today should result in a sustainable world seven generations into the future'. I think that's a great place to start.

Clare Honeyfield, 2021

Alex Merry

ARTIST

From global city-centre murals to Morris dancing for Hot Chip at Glastonbury Festival, Alex Merry is not your typical rural artisan, if such a thing even exists. Well known for her exquisite illustrations for Gucci and for founding Boss Morris, Alex grew up in a vicarage in the centre of Stroud, one of three siblings raised on a modest priest's income while being surrounded by art and culture.

The whole family of three kids managed to each pass the application for a bursary to get a scholarship to Wycliffe School in Stonehouse, which Alex describes as a 'crazily privileged and academic education. We were so lucky to have the opportunity.'

'I've always loved painting at home; it was just second nature,' says Alex, whose mum is an artist. 'My family are a huge inspiration to me. My mum is a self-taught artist and one of my earliest memories is sitting on her desk watching her paint with colourful inks. My childhood is still my greatest influence – from the books that Mum and Dad read to us, to the imaginary world my brother, sister and I created. I love "outsider" artists – people who create obsessively and compulsively, whether anyone sees their work or not. Traditional crafts are another really big influence and I draw a lot of inspiration from British folk culture. I'd be way more excited learning how to weave a corn dolly than I would exhibiting in a swanky art gallery!'

Alex had to fight hard for her creative A-level choices of art, music and history of art, and was encouraged at school to apply to study an academic degree in history of art. Once at university, she was often to be found drawing portraits of students in the halls, 'I was desperate to do practical art'.

Alex accepted that the course wasn't for her and returned home to attend the art foundation course at Stroud College. Here, Alex describes enthusiastically how she became instantly inspired by the teaching and international trips. Highlights included her first ever experience of travelling outside Europe to visit Luxor in Egypt with the college.

Alex went on to study illustration in Bristol, at the University of the West of England (UWE), following the suggestion of the tutors at Stroud College, partly because she wanted to immerse herself in techniques rather than being steered in the direction of more conceptual work. Alex found herself totally engaged in the course, developing her love of painting, learning the craft of illustration, life drawing, portraits and observational studies and discovering the practicalities of using different materials.

Like so many students, university for Alex was all about finding her tribe and hanging around town with fellow students doing observational drawings in railways stations, parks and public spaces. She amazingly got a commission to illustrate a children's book at this time but, as for many creative undergraduates, she didn't earn enough as an artist to make a living. Upon completing her degree, Alex stayed in Bristol doing care work and working with young people.

After a few years, Alex returned to Stroud and started working for Damien Hirst at Science, something she describes as a big chapter of her life. 'Working at Science was exciting and socially nourishing; a brilliant experience in many unexpected ways, working with other artists in the studio, becoming confident with oil painting, and helping to set up a studio in London for a big exhibition – all really formative experiences.'

While living and working in London for Hirst, Alex discovered Cecil Sharp House in Camden, the centre of English folk dance and song, which housed a library of recordings, books and everything folky. Alex got into the Morris dancing scene, something she fondly remembers her dad doing at home in her childhood – hopping around in the dining room with big white handkerchiefs causing everything on the dresser to shake and the dresser doors to open.

Attending dancing classes at Cecil Sharp House, she became 'obsessed'. Dancing with mainly older people, Alex was inspired to set up The Belles of London City, an all-women's rather funky Morris side, with two friends. She describes delving into the rootsy traditions of English folklore as being an escape from the intense world of commercial art production. At this time, Alex was employed making photorealist oil paintings and worked for a couple of prominent artists but, like many creatives, found the city lifestyle hard to maintain.

Alex moved back to Stroud, describing moving out of London as being 'like stepping off the merry-go-round'. Initially intending to stay in Stroud only temporarily, Alex started working for Darbyshire Frame Makers, spending her time acclimatising to rural life again. She enjoyed the craft-based nature of the work.

She ended up project managing a big collaborative enterprise for a highly successful international artist, learning lots of new skills, but when the project came to an end, Alex began getting into her own creativity again and painted a stylised portrait of her parents' cats as a Christmas gift. She really enjoyed the process and the freedom, along with what she describes as the 'slightly kitsch and rather uncool nature' of the work after intensely working in commercial art.

Commissions for fantasy pet portraits followed and Alex was back to being a freelance artist, supporting herself through bar work at Stroud Valleys Artspace. She continued to paint family

portraits in her free time, developing her folk-art style, building a portfolio and publishing her work on her social media account.

Alex really loved the fact that she was painting pet portraits – not necessarily considered 'art' – as she hates art snobbery and loves animals and the process of honouring the relationship that people have with their pets. 'A lot of my work is commission based, so my paintings are a collaboration between myself and the client. That's partly what drew me to studying illustration as I like working to a brief. It helps me explore subject matters and methods that I'd probably never arrive at by myself. The pet portraits are a great example of that and I love dreaming up an image with the person commissioning the painting.'

Completely out of the blue, Alex got an email from Gucci, who had discovered her work on Instagram. After initially thinking the email was a hoax, Alex was offered a collaboration with the design house and set to work researching their new collections. Alex's first commission was for Gucci DIY, painting A5 cards for their customised clothing ranges. Alex had ten days to do twenty-one paintings and worked night and day.

She then got a contract working for Gucci Décor, and developed a new style of painting in layers and digitalising her work to make it easily changeable for the client. This accidental discovery of a new working style felt like a massive step forward for Alex, who paints oils onto offcuts of wooden boards and works digitally with her originals.

The Gucci Garden wanted a series of murals to go up the staircase of their museum to show a metaphysical interpretation of the main square in Florence. Gucci had a team of painters who came in at night to paint Alex's designs onto the walls while the venue was closed, as the work needed to be completed in a week. Alex's designs were also used for Gucci screensavers, downloads and patches for Gucci DIY as well as in their social media as animations. 'I find seeing my work painted on the side of a wall in New York completely and utterly surreal. The Gucci Art Walls popped up all over the world and it completely boggled my brain when photos of them started appearing on social media. I went to see one of the murals in London and stood underneath it for ages trying to register it. I was lucky enough to meet some of the painters who did the giant murals and they're so skilled at what they do. The whole experience has been amazing.'

Boss Morris runs alongside Alex's painting and illustration, gaining a global reputation itself. As a group, the dancers design and make their own costumes, dance traditional dances and have reinvented Morris dancing for our time. Well known for their unique style and energy, the group were invited to dance for Hot Chip at Glastonbury Festival, after being introduced to them by Lauren Lavern, who is a massive fan, on BBC Radio 6 Music. Alex says, 'I have always thought that Morris is the key to the universe; it unlocks all these experiences that I would never have dreamt of.'

Alex continues to live and paint in Stroud, and Boss Morris meet on Painswick Beacon, Rodborough Common and other hills at pivotal times of the year, solstices and equinoxes, bringing their unique magic to the valleys. 'I'm naturally quite a hermit so I really love the feeling of being "in the zone", painting with music on and the cat snoring in the chair next to me. That's blissful for me.'

www.alexmerryart.com

Instagram: @alexmerryart

Annie Hutchinson

TEXTILE SCULPTOR

- Little Wren House Factory -

To walk into Annie's studio is to walk into another world, where pug dogs wear petticoats, cats go shopping and wooden cotton reels become the bases for felted bird automata. The whole space is full of bright colours, deep tones, vintage fabrics and miniatures, and works in progress, as well as shelves of the most incredible creatures, finished and waiting for a new home, collectibles, and unusual and colourful objects.

Annie herself is a work of art, with candy pink hair decorated with scarves and silk flowers, bold vintage brooches and rings, layers of costume-like clothing and traditional handmade clogs, assembled with the utmost flair and imagination. She is often to be found, basket over arm, early in the morning enjoying the delights of the Vintage Mary stall in the Shambles Market in Stroud, from where she sources many of the accessories and fabrics for her creations.

So, what led to a career making exquisitely dressed dolls with felted animal heads, automata and ephemera?

Annie was brought up in the Welsh valleys, in what she describes as a 'cultural and artistic wilderness'. 'Even though I didn't have anyone in my life to inspire or encourage me, I always drew and made things as a child – sometimes scratching images into the furniture to the exasperation of my mother!'

Annie has distinct memories of trying to make clothes for her dolls by cutting, wrapping and tying fabrics, having not yet discovered stitching. 'At the age of 7, I decided I wanted to go to art college. I don't even know how I knew art college existed – possibly my older brother told me about it.'

Annie finally achieved this in 1985, doing a foundation course at Cardiff Art College. Having started out doing painting and drawing, by the end of the course Annie had discovered a love for working three dimensionally. This led her to studying fine art sculpture at Cheltenham, a three-year degree, where she discovered an affiliation with textiles, producing soft sculptures for her final show.

After graduating, Annie got a Prince's Trust grant for ceramics equipment and a kiln for a studio in the basement at Axiom Art Centre in Cheltenham; the Tribe were in the next studio. Annie exhibited at Stuttgart Festival, South Wales Potters, and carried out a number of private commissions.

Annie still created while taking time out to have children. She and her family ended up living in Stroud because she was homesick for Wales, but her husband's job didn't allow him to move there. She cites the Welsh term 'hiraeth', a longing, homesickness, and a feeling of missing the mountains. Stroud fed the need for landscape, and Annie says she loves living here as it is so diverse and accepting: 'Stroud feels like a safe place full of artists and creatives.'

Having always been into antiques, Annie moved into china restoration for a while and then ventured into doll making, producing her first in 2007. With her youngest now in school, she joined an evening knitting circle but wasn't, she says, 'very much of a knitter' and only managed to make a tea cosy and a scarf before deciding to make a doll instead. She bought felting needles for the hair and then went on to make a needle-felted bird.

From here she got the idea to make needle-felted heads for her dolls. She attended a felting course in Stroud town centre with Margaret Docherty and started making felt wall pieces which were sold in Made in Stroud. Extending the combination of doll making and needle felting, Annie started making anthropomorphic dolls, setting up The Little Wren House Factory in 2008.

Annie's typical working day starts at 6 a.m., and she describes herself as organising herself and the family, getting out of the house by 8 a.m. Having worked from home for ten years, Annie took a studio space in the Painswick Inn, Stroud, in 2020. 'I like the walk from Whiteshill village, where I live, into Stroud, a 2-mile journey across fields with spectacular views across the five valleys.'

She tends, she says, to work on several pieces at once, having worked out the character and title of each piece with some preliminary drawings and note making. She next turns her attention to making the 'skins', as she refers to them, or the bodies, out of calico, which is pre-dyed to give it an aged patina. The patterns for the bodies are her own, made in various sizes and shapes so she has a selection to choose from. These 'skins' are then stitched and stuffed. 'I find working with thread and stitch a gentle meditative process with gives me the time to develop my ideas for the piece.'

Annie uses a range of techniques, from machine stitching, dying, fabric painting and needle felting to decoupage and varnishing for her wooden pieces. Any number of these processes could be used in a working day at the studio. 'Life can be so fast and demanding, when I'm stitching in my studio, all is well with the world.'

Annie's inspirations come from her love of old things – her home is beautifully crammed with interesting objects and curios. 'I have magpie-like tendencies, not only collecting materials and bric-a-brac to use in my work but also for my home, which is a megalomaniac mix of the strange and the unwanted, that have been collected over the last thirty years. This stuff never ceases to be an inspiration to me.'

The inspiration for her animal heads (which, unusually, sit on the bodies of disproportioned, handmade dolls that have been dressed in her distinctive style) comes from childhood pets, favourite childhood stories such as *Brer Rabbit* and *Wind in the Willows*, as well as fairy stories and fables. Her work is sometimes autobiographical, showing the irony and humour in daily situations. She also takes inspiration from folk art, such as George Smart's collaged figures of village folk and the drawings of Arthur Rackham.

Annie also has a passion for nineteenth-century French toys, curios and automata, and she is always working on ideas of how to incorporate movement in the form of simple automata, jumping jacks, puppets, marionettes and old taxidermy. Her love of colour, surface texture and patterns is evident in her work, which is predominantly about putting different images together to make a completely new one.

'To recycle and reuse is very important to me. If I need a particular material, I always scout the charity shops and visit car boots to try and source what I want. We are very lucky to have the wonderful resource of Vintage Mary at the Shambles Market where I can pick up almost anything you could want – and if they haven't got it, they will find it for you – just wonderful!' Annie is always on the lookout for materials and bits and pieces to make her mixed media work: 'I am always going on searching expeditions. This can be locally, in Stroud charity shops, and as I've mentioned, Vintage Mary's stall is always a great source for useful ephemera, whether it's vintage, retro or purely the discarded. Flea markets such as Malvern and Shepton Mallet are also a great source for materials.

'This also applies to the cottage in which I live. Most, if not all, have been found in such places or bought on eBay. Living in a small town like Stroud, sometimes you pick up information from the community, or even while enjoying a coffee in a café, about things that are no longer wanted. One case in point is our 1950s 'English Rose' kitchen. Through a conversation struck up across a café table we managed to purchase the kitchen units and are laboriously stripping away the old, tired paint by hand to reveal the shiny metal underneath. A true labour of love but very rewarding and so cool.'

The cottage is eclectic. To the outsider it may seem rather random and haphazard but on closer examination everything has its rightful place, whether that's a painted plate on the black conservatory wall or a puppet or toy in the 'Cabinet of Delights' in the snug. 'I very much feel that as my art mimics life so does my life mimic my art. They are one and the same, and I am most happy living this way.'

Annie's work is widely exhibited at shows, events and venues including Made by Hand, the Hay Festival, SIT Select, based in Stroud, the Made in Stroud shop and several national galleries. Her work can also be found in several private collections.

www.thelittlewrenhousefactory.co.uk

Instagram: @littlewrenhouse
Email: andynette@tiscali.co.uk

Bridget Williams

POTTER

Bridget Williams is a well-known Stroud potter, who is loved for her blue and white spotty and microblue-patterned domestic ware. Bridget's mugs and vessels grace many a dresser in the Cotswolds and beyond. Describing pottery as 'kind of what I do', Bridget says, 'The best bit is the throwing'.

Walking to Bridget's home along a brick footpath, I am struck by the landscape. Her house is tucked away in a hidden valley, with stunning views and an unusual peace. Like many artists, Bridget has built a studio in her garden, just steps away from her back door. The studio houses pots at various stages of production, from slip-decorated mugs and plates drying out for their first firing to bisque-fired pots waiting to be glazed and fired. A room in her home contains walls lined with shelves of completed pieces, ready to go out to shops and galleries.

Bridget threw her first pot as a student at Liverpool Polytechnic, studying for a fine art degree in painting and printmaking. She was, she says, 'never really a painter', but wasn't sure what to specialise in after her foundation year, and was advised to 'do what your friends are doing'. During the summer term, when the graduates' work was on show in the studios, Bridget says, 'I invited myself to the ceramics department which was part of the sculpture department – completely separate from the fine art painting studios. I helped myself to some clay, put it on the wheel and proceeded to try throwing a pot. With no supervision and no knowledge of the craft, I had chosen a clay which is much too gritty to throw and ended up grazing the skin off

the side of my hand and making my whole hand raw.' That was Bridget's first throwing – she didn't make anything, she just ground the skin off her hand.

Apart from a small project to build a clay head in her foundation year, this was Bridget's only experience of working with clay as an art student. When she went on to study art therapy, there was a small clay project to make two pinch pots, join them together and burnish them, doing a bonfire firing in sawdust. The finished piece looked like shiny pewter. 'Hand building and raku firing sowed a little seed that was the beginning of the organic shapes and the hand building, my secret passion.'

Working as a play therapist at Great Ormond Street Children's Hospital in London, with an emphasis on arts and crafts, Bridget began attending night classes at Morley College, taught by Naine Woodrow, co-founder of North Street Potters in Clapham, a collective of makers with their own shop front. Bridget focused on her love of hand building. After a few years of evening classes, under the supervision of Naine, Bridget began to learn throwing, on the understanding that 'you are going to throw away all of your pots for a term'.

On reflection, Bridget says this was a great way to learn, as her technique would improve so much week to week that firing any of her attempts would have resulted in owning 'disappointingly wonky pots'. She still shares this story with her pottery students today. After a few terms, Naine asked Bridget, 'Would you like to be a proper potter?' Bridget took a deep breath, said, 'Yes', rented Naine's workspace while Naine went back to Australia for the summer, and got potting.

Bridget went on to work a job share in a children's centre, while making pots on the kitchen table at home, and from then, the pottery work gradually took more and more days and the play work fewer days. Eventually finding her niche as a slip decorator, Bridget learned about packing a tight kiln and improved her throwing, also revelling in helping in the shop.

Bridget moved out of London when she was taken on as the Potter in Residence at Prema Arts Centre in Uley, in 1988, and her partner James, a painter, got a teaching job in Bristol. This is when Bridget started using terracotta, an earthenware clay which is lighter, more orange and fired at a lower temperature than stoneware.

Incredibly, Bridget still has a collection of her original stoneware plates and bowls from her time at North Street Potters. Her experimentation with surface patterns using paper cuts and brush strokes can be seen in these pieces. In fact, Bridget's kitchen is like a museum to her craft, cataloguing every stage of the evolution of the process, right up to today's experimentation with a potential new range of grey and yellow slips and patterns. Early styles included using wax resist, drawing, torn paper strips and building up interesting surfaces on stoneware, the house clay at North Street Potters.

Bridget and James initially lived in a rented cottage, which they shared with agricultural students. 'We gradually worked out that Stroud was the place to be and moved to Stroud to settle down and have a family.' Bridget took some time off from making but continued to play with patterns and materials in her craft as soon as she was able.

Bridget's working week is variable, but surprisingly structured, and begins with a cup of tea and a walk or cycle ride before breakfast, starting in the studio mid-morning and working through until early evening up to seven days a week, popping back to her garden studio in the evening to move things as they dry. I ask Bridget how she copes with the cold in the studio, having her hands in wet clay all day. 'Organisation is key. I work around kiln firings, which happen every other week, on the whole. The day before and the day after firings, the studio is warmed by the kiln getting up to heat and cooling down. In winter, I go to the studio wearing ski trousers and body warmers and I boil a kettle to take with me so I can use warm water while throwing on the wheel.'

Hating waste, Bridget packs the kiln tightly for the initial bisque firing, stacking candle holders inside mugs, for example. For the glaze firing, it is important that nothing touches, so there are two glaze firings to every bisque. In between firings the kiln is used as a drying cupboard for the clay to dry it faster on damp winter days.

'Hand building and raku firing sowed a little seed that was the beginning of the organic shapes and the hand building, my secret passion.'

Bridget seems to be continually trying out new methods of creating patterns and is currently working on a new style and colourway but says she is spending too much time on each piece and needs to simplify to make the new range commercially viable. The new range is grey, because over the years people have visited the studio, seen the pots before they had been fired and said, 'Oh, I love that grey'. It was, however, grey slip that turned to a deep, dark blue in the glaze firing, so after a few years of thinking about it, Bridget has developed a new range and has named it 'Retrogrey'.

Bridget continues with her hand building, which she concentrates on in January after the Christmas rush of making stock for shops, creating smooth organic sea pod and shell-like forms which she exhibits at Oxford Artweeks and various shows around the UK. Bridget had been teaching pottery classes regularly until the pandemic and has commitments to work in various collective shops where she sells her work.

So why blue? 'When I started working with earthenware at Prema I just loved the contrast between the terracotta clay and the glazed blue slip – they are opposite colours.'

Bridget is also a musician, playing flute and accordion, and is in a band with her partner James, who plays double bass. Their band played at the launch of Stroud Farmers' Market in 1999 and were part of the Stroud Community Play in 1991. Over the years, Bridget has taught in various schools and colleges around Stroud and designed and created a ceramic totem pole at a local primary school with the children and teachers.

Bridget's work is incredibly popular and widely collected. You can find her pottery for sale at the Made in Stroud shop, Potters in Bristol, the Gloucestershire Guild Shop in Cheltenham, New Brewery Arts in Cirencester and North Street Potters in London, and you can visit her studio during Open Studios in Stroud.

www.bridgetwilliams.co.uk
Instagram: @bridgetwilliams_ceramics
Email: bridgetannewilliams@gmail.com

Charlie Clarke

POTTER

- *Little Earthquake Pots* -

Visiting Charlie is like entering another world. It's a spring day; I park my car and walk through the gates to her pottery where I am greeted by the dogs. From the gently sloping garden on the sunny side of a valley, walking through buttercups, the grass wet with the morning dew, the vast valley below seems to stretch on forever, and all that can be heard is birdsong and the wind in the leaves of the surrounding woodland.

Charlie's tiny studio is a traditional log cabin construction, built for her by her partner Will using timber from Woodchester Park which Will felled himself. Ivy the dog is curled up by the burner in her fluffy dog bed. There's a roaring fire in the burner and a pot of jasmine tea on the stove top. The sun pours in through the window and racks of pots are at various stages of drying around the walls.

In front of the studio and down the hill is the traditional Scandinavian-style larch log cabin that Will built for them to live in. He designed and built the cabin from a book and has since been on a course and now builds log cabins. The cabins are super cosy, insulated with sheep wool and are incredibly peaceful. Their home is entirely off-grid with a UV rainwater filtration system and solar panels, and it sits on the side of a stunning valley, with no roads or houses in sight. Charlie tells me that when she moved in, she found the cabin rather dark, so Will got a chainsaw and cut a large hole in the end wall and put a window in it – thoroughly handmade.

Charlie's original career was in broadcast journalism, working in radio and music magazines. Her mum is very creative and did a lot of sculpture, which Charlie says gave her a confidence with clay. As a child in Nottinghamshire, she'd always enjoyed painting and drawing and would play with clay, although she was never formally trained.

It was at an evening class in 2010 in a club called Ox Pots in Oxford that Charlie fell in love with pottery. 'In that evening class, I experienced a nostalgia for working with clay as a material and felt like, "Wow, I've just got to do this, I cannot NOT do this!"' Charlie says that, from that moment, she was bitten by the bug and wanted to learn more. There wasn't a throwing teacher, so Charlie tried to teach herself, 'struggling away on a wheel', as she describes it, and hand building.

Wanting to learn more, Charlie booked some lessons with Canadian potter Caroline Haurie, who was living in the UK at the time. Charlie was so enthusiastic that she told her teacher she wanted to make a five-year plan to become a professional potter. Caroline totally supported Charlie in this idea and encouraged her to find apprenticeships.

A potter she met at Oxford Ceramics Fair, Richard Phethean, suggested trying Whichford Pottery near Chipping Norton,

'The clay absorbs everything. You can't make a good pot if you are angry, you have to be centred, grounded and in the moment. If I'm not in the right space for potting I go and do some clay recycling'

which made incredible giant flowerpots, some of which, Charlie says, you could stand inside. 'At the time I was pestering for a job, Whichford had a third-generation Japanese potter apprenticing for them. Kazuya Ishida was incredibly skilled at throwing and has an impressive ceramics heritage. He had just announced that he was leaving them and going back to Japan earlier than planned. I was very lucky to have been in the right place at the right time, but in no way filled the talent gap he left.'

Charlie describes herself as spending a year mucking in with every job that needed doing, from vacuuming around and under the potters' chairs to loading kilns, wedging clay and making tiles and cane tops. In the evenings and at weekends she would stay and throw hundreds of 'practice pots'. Occasionally, some of the senior potters would stay on and teach a bit. It wasn't a formal apprenticeship but an invaluable learning experience.

After having to take six months off with illness, Charlie took on a job at the Ashmolean Museum, showing people around the ceramics galleries. She also volunteered for the royal warrant holder Mia Sarosi, who works with porcelain, and taught courses for an American potter, Katie Costen of Illyria Pottery, in exchange for the use of the studio.

Charlie was just getting her business set up and was starting to get commissions when she met Will. 'Will said, "If you move out here I'll build you a studio." While I was getting set up, I took a job at the local deli to pay the bills and learned fish mongering!' When they got Ivy as a puppy, Charlie needed to be at home to look after her and took the opportunity to work long hours establishing her ceramics business.

Throwing pots is a very physical job and quite demanding emotionally but not terribly demanding intellectually. Charlie describes centring the pot on the wheel as an opportunity to centre yourself. This is the first part of the process of making a pot. She says, 'The clay needs you to be grounded for it. The clay absorbs everything. You can't make a good pot if you are angry. You have to be centred, grounded and in the moment. If I'm not in the right space for potting I go and do some clay recycling.'

Charlie says you also have to be careful what music you listen to when you are throwing – classical music and reggae are good. She also listens to a lot of audio books and art history while she is throwing, she says, 'to keep in perspective what I am doing and why'. At the time of the interview, she is listening to a series about the Renaissance history of Italy. Having background music or audio going on 'when you're in the sweet spot flow of the physical side' enables the muscle memory to take over and reduces overthinking. Then you can throw multiples of the same pot that you've trained your muscles to make, which is really useful for production pottery. If you are making a run for a large order, you can take your mind out of the equation and just let your body take over.'

Charlie's kilns and glazes are housed in another outside barn building and her glazes are unusual. Bright sunshine yellows, deep reds and warm oranges are her signature glazes for her popular noodle bowls, mugs and large vases. She uses cobalt and iron blue for the drawings on her illustrated pieces. Cobalt is known as the 'gentleman' of the oxides as it is very forgiving and very tolerant of a wide range of firing temperatures. Orange is a more difficult colour to create, using a lot of oxides and stains balanced with frit.

Charlie has managed to create an orange colour using a reduction technique, starving the kiln of oxygen at nearly the top temperature for a few hundred degrees, which changes the colour from a green to a red or an orange. However, all the oxides make the glaze very runny, so she has added a calcium chloride 'frit' which suspends the molecules and make it less runny – glazes are such a science and making glazes is 'a bit of alchemy'. Also, because she uses a real flame gas-fired kiln, which she converted from electric, there is a differentiation in temperature that affects the colour and texture of each finished piece. Charlie has a whole library of glaze manuals and notebooks in the barn, and her glazes are not just admired by customers. When she took her pots to Hatfield, Windsor and Farnham Art in Clay, events that host a few hundred ceramic artists, she got some great feedback from her fellow potters.

Charlie points out that ceramics is taught as an art subject but the chemistry of the glazes, the physics of the kiln building, numeracy, literacy and the business acumen needed to become a commercially successful potter makes it a thoroughly practical career with applied sciences.

Through her 'Clay Dates', Charlie teaches pottery in the studio. These are popular for couples, mums and sons, or friends who want to learn a bit about throwing, and make great 'experience' gifts. Guests come and sit in the cabin studio and after a couple of hours of tuition in throwing, the resulting pots are left with Charlie to fire and glaze them. 'It's a lovely low-pressure way to see if pottery is for you, or just a lovely escape from life,' she says. She describes the class as an 'active mindfulness', a facilitated meditative experience where people can leave the outside world behind and just be in the moment, create something and be in a safe, friendly, private, space. Some people have used it for getting through grief or a self-art therapy. 'It's just you and the clay', says Charlie, and the environment up here really is an escape.

Charlie sells through Burford Garden Company, the Iona Gallery in Woodstock, the Made in Stroud shop, Stroud Farmers' Market and Eastington Farm Shop, and she also welcomes private commissions through Instagram.

www.littleearthquakepots.com

Instagram: @littleearthquakepots
Facebook: 'Clay Date'

Dave Cockcroft

CHAIRMAKER

Like many homes in Stroud, Dave has a garden shed, and it is here he finishes off making his chairs. Stepping inside, the walls are hung with ready-formed spindles, legs and seats for chairs. A cupboard on the wall holds an array of specialist carving implements and bark hangs in curls to be used for seating. There are letterpress posters by Dennis Gould, who was for some years a lodger in the family home and is also featured in this book. Wood shavings line the floor and the sun shines in through the windows from the garden.

Originally a web designer, Dave was the designer of the first websites for Stroud Farmers' Market and the Made in Stroud shop. He became interested in green woodwork when visiting Ruskin Mill, where he attended a taster day. He had seen leaflets at Westonbirt for courses and had always wanted to learn more, so when the kids were teenagers, he attended his first chairmaking courses in 2006 at the Cherry Wood Project at Marshfield, near Bath.

His first project was a three-legged stool, then he made a shave horse, followed by a chair with a woven seat. He started chairmaking seriously in 2014 and has been focussed on Welsh stick chairs since 2016. He also makes spoons, teaches spoon carving and makes specialist spoon-carving tools. He's known online as 'Davethebodger', 'bodger' being an old word for folks who worked in the woods making parts for chairs.

'I had a transition phase while I was still designing websites part time, and this was a hobby, so a lot of my learning was when I was in hobby mode. I made all our dining chairs, chairs for friends, and used to make other styles and traditions of greenwood furniture. One of the things I like about the Welsh stick chairs is that they are very simple, but if you get them right, they are very elegant.'

As Dave explains, the garden shed workshop is used only for finishing his work, which he prepares elsewhere. He sources his main material, timber, from local wood yards, Westonbirt Arboretum and from people who have trees they need to cut down in their gardens locally.

Dave loves to work outside and shares a woodyard out of town, from where he does the preliminary work on his chairs. He starts with air-dried elm planks for the seats and oak or ash for legs and spindles, all native hardwoods. The trunk is used as the main material for his pieces, because of the straight grain and strength. At the yard, he works outside, cutting and shaping seats, legs and backs for the chairs, initially cutting to length and splitting the trunk pieces and then shaping with hand tools. The wood is prepared green, while it is softest and easiest to work, then brought back to his garden shed for finishing.

'I start off with a piece of trunk that might be a foot wide and several feet long. The sticks aren't made from a branch because if you have a skinny branch with the pith in – the very middle bit of the wood, which is soft – you tend to get cracking and it's not so strong. If you start with a bigger piece of wood and split it, and lose the middle, you get a stronger and longer-lasting piece of furniture. When green, fresh-cut, that is, ash and oak are good for splitting along their length.'

Dave splits the trunks with an axe and wedges until he has maybe eight pieces from a trunk, then he uses a tool called a 'froe' and a 'cleaving break', which is a way of making a controlled split so that the sticks are the same width top and bottom. The sticks are thicker for legs and longer and thinner for spindles and are refined on a shave horse using a drawknife – a really satisfying process. He carefully works them thinner but leaves the green parts slightly oversized to allow for shrinkage as they dry.

'When I come to assemble a chair, I have a set of sticks which I put in the drying cupboard for a few days to force any remaining moisture out, then I do a bit more work to final dimensions, either on the shave horse or in the vice.'

The final part of the process is when he tapers the sticks to just the right width to fit into the back of the chairs where they slot through the arm bow. This tapering and thinning gives the chair backs a bit of 'spring' which makes it more comfortable.

There is some steam bending involved in making a chair. 'There isn't much other than the crest, or it's sometimes called the comb, at the top of the chair that I steam bend. Sometimes I steam bend the arm as well, but it's tricky to find knot-free, straight-grained wood for this. Traditionally, in this way of making, people didn't have steamers so they would have used naturally curved pieces of wood or would have sawn a curve out of a thicker piece. I don't do that as it's hard to source the right naturally curved pieces of wood.'

Making the legs for the chair is similar but the wood is thicker. The bottom of the legs is wider, which Dave says gives a design feeling of the furniture being 'rooted' into the ground, like tree trunks. The legs are hexagonal or octagonal, which catches the light nicely. The tenons, where the legs fit through holes in the seat, are sized to fit perfectly using a rotary plane. Most parts are finished with a draw knife or plane, so the whole chair is carved rather than using any lathe-turned components. Long, straight grain means that the back sticks can be quite thin and will bend like a fishing rod without breaking.

The legs are set into the seat with more rake and splay than is typical in English Windsor chairs, giving them a more dynamic appearance. The tapered legs are held into the seat with wedges to keep them secure. This is then trimmed off and scraped to a smooth finish. Once the seat is assembled, the arm spindles can be added. Drilling all the holes at the correct angles is one of the trickiest parts of the whole process but vital for a comfortable and good-looking chair.

Dave enjoys the process of making, describing the joy of not having to use power tools, protective clothing or ear protection and being able to work outside in nature. Working with hand tools is a safe and environmentally friendly way to work. Being made outside from green wood with hand tools makes the chairs incredibly eco, although he does use a drying cabinet on the timber before assembling, to ensure that the chair lasts a long time in a centrally heated home.

Ash is a much more blonde wood, while oak and elm are darker in tone and generally more favoured by customers. Chairs can be finished in natural colour or turned black like many of the old Welsh stick chairs. Most of the chairs Dave makes are sold to houses in Wales. The black is achieved by ebonising with an iron acetate solution made by dissolving iron filings in vinegar. This reacts with the tannin in the wood to create iron tannate, dying the wood black. This process would have been used with oak galls (oak apples) to create ink for writing on manuscripts by scribes in the distant past.

'The Welsh stick chair is a very democratic chair, not traditionally made by specialist makers, and would have been made in the countryside by farmers, carpenters, wheelwrights or anyone who had a few tools before the mass production of furniture. They used to be very common in Wales and have seen a resurgence of interest in recent years,' says Dave. The chairs are beautiful, long lasting and are purchased as heirlooms. He finds his commissions are often for wedding gifts, birthday presents and retirement gifts. His chairs are widely regarded as heirloom-quality items which will last for generations.

Dave also runs spoon-carving courses at the Woodyard and in a yurt in a friend's orchard. Using his knowledge of spoon carving, he makes specialist carving knives which are sold to whittlers all around the world. He obtains rough-forged bearing steel blades from a blacksmith in Wales and then shapes and sharpens them on a linisher, making handles from elm offcuts from the chair seats, and then makes woven sheaths from birch bark. Like his chairs, he has a waiting list for his knives and will usually list a batch of knives through his website, often selling out overnight to his waiting list.

'I make a lot of dolphin spoons, which is a traditional Welsh style of eating spoon, and *cawl* spoons, "*cawl*" being Welsh for soup or stew.' He also makes a lot of coffee scoops and cups when he has time. He finds spoon carving relaxing and usually keeps the spoons he makes until he has a big batch. He will then put them all up on his website, where the whole lot will sell quickly to carvers and collectors all over the world.

Most of Dave's furniture commissions and orders come through his Instagram account, where he uploads lots of short videos and instructional tutorials.

www.davecockcroft.co.uk

Instagram: @davethebodger

Dennis Gould

WRITER AND LETTERPRESS PRINTER

~ *The Woodblock Letterpress* ~

Dennis can be seen every Sunday cycling up the steep, winding hill to his local, the Woolpack, for a hearty home-cooked roast and a pint overlooking Laurie Lee's Slad Valley. Writer, performance poet, keen cyclist, anarchist and letterpress printer, he is well known for his distinctive letterpress prints. 'I'm a writer first and a letterpress printer second,' he says, in his proud Derbyshire accent.

A lifelong peace campaigner, philosopher and alternative academic, Dennis began performing as a Riff Raff poet with his friends Jeff Cloves and Miss Pat West at the St Ives Festival in 1970. Occasionally they would be accompanied by musician friends, inspired by the founding fathers of jazz poetry, Laurence Ferlinghetti, Kenneth Rexroth and Kenneth Patchen. He corresponded with Lawrence Ferlinghetti from 1964 until his death in 2021, aged 101 and 11 months, and used to perform his poetry.

Coming from a working-class background in Burton-on-Trent, Dennis has, among other things, trained as a map maker in the army, been arrested and imprisoned for non-violent direct action at an air base, served a prison sentence, during which time he got books sent in for the prison library, managed a peace café, been a van driver in London and studied at Woodbrook Quaker College in Birmingham. He has also worked as an international volunteer, distribution editor for *Peace News* in the time of manual typewritten lists, and a community worker offering benefits and housing advice with Uhuru Community Café in Cowley Road, Oxford, opposite the famous wholefood shop of the same name.

It was while driving a furniture removal van around London that Dennis discovered Kenneth Patchen of City Lights Books in San Francisco, a leading light and founding father of the American jazz poetry scene. Dennis was so inspired by his work that he wrote to Kenneth via his publishers to ask if he could publish a collection of his poems. Even though he had no experience in this, Dennis got permission and eventually printed the collection in 1968 onto matt paper with letterpress. He would spend time in the British Museum researching Patchen's writings and got copies of City Lights and New Directions books sent from America. The collection was called *Love and War Poems*.

About twenty people made donations to the cost of the printing and Dennis printed their names on the cover. He sent off a handful of review copies, and his work got picked up and reviewed by P.J. Kavanagh in the *Guardian* alongside Patchen's *Collected Poems* by Jonathan Cape, which Dennis didn't know was being published. In the same review was a book of poems by Adrian Mitchell. 'I think of Adrian Mitchell as the unofficial Poet Laureate and one of the finest poets of his generation, as well as being one of the founders of performance poetry, going to colleges and schools. Alongside Michael Horovitz and Christopher Logue, they brought poetry alive. Nowadays in Stroud we have Elvis McGonagall and Adam Horovitz. There are now performers all over the country which didn't happen much in the sixties.'

From the review in the *Guardian* in 1967, Dennis got orders for his pamphlet, and at the time he had started to do readings in schools and teacher training colleges in the day and at folk clubs, working men's clubs, CND meetings, demonstrations, festivals and Quaker meetings in the evenings and at weekends. He began to get more bookings for educational establishments and would travel the country by coach, which he describes as 'cheap but very stuffy', being put up by hosts in the towns he was performing/reading in.

'I started printing by chance in 1991. I had been producing postcards and posters since the sixties. I came to Stroud to go to John Marjoram's fiftieth birthday party and stayed here. I went to see John Grice of Evergreen Press at Piccadilly Mill, to ask him to print a postcard I'd written about the Save the Trees campaign in Stratford Park. I came back a few weeks later and he'd been too busy to do it. He had a Derby Treadle Platen press and said I could use that to try to print them. It took me seven hours to set the very first letters I'd ever done, and it was a fourteen-line poem. I printed about 150 copies of "Stroud Eye View Blues" and got hooked. I was printing my own words and the words of people I admired.'

Just two weeks later, Dennis bought his own second-hand letterpress and some type a couple of weeks after that, which John let him put in his workshop. He printed there for a couple of years and then eventually rented a tiny, shared studio in Stroud Valleys Artspace until the renovations took place, when everyone moved from one temporary studio to another. He moved to his present studio in 2010.

'I'd been around letterpress printers all my life but I'd never done it. When you are outside a craft, it looks complicated. It's essentially simple, but the art is in the layout. The thing that takes the time is the typesetting, because you are setting individual lead letters.' Dennis goes on to explain the most important part of the process: 'You put the letters into a compositor's stick that is set to the width you want, and when you have your line you get your piece of leading, you put that onto the compositor's stick, turn the whole line over, so the individual letters rest on the leading, press your thumbs, lift it out and put it into the galley where you are printing. You do this line by line while holding the compositor's stick at 45 degrees so the letters don't fall out. After some hours, you have your printing plate ready.'

WhiteWayColony

For Those In Love

For All Those In Sane

StroudWaterCanal

For All those in Pain

For All those in Prison

19 96

ToadsMoorValley

PainsWick Beacon

For All Those In Love

For All Those In Sane

It would be true to say that each plate Dennis creates is a work of art in itself. His choice of font, layout and illustrative 'blocks' are as distinctive as his unique writing and views of life. 'Over the years I bought cases of type from other printers, and blocks, which are the illustrations. You can still get blocks made of any photograph or illustration; there are still block-makers around. The blocks are made of hardwood with metal tacked on, are "type high", which is an inch high. Everything has to be at the same height. The letters are made from 98.5 per cent lead and 1.5 per cent antinomy, which helps the lead to harden. Printers' ink is traditionally oil based although more environmentally friendly alternatives are now available. 'When I started, I used any scraps of paper, and I swore I'd never use handmade paper, but I now use almost all handmade paper made from recycled cotton rag, as it sets off the letterpress nicely. I also print onto recycled maps and onto fabric. Milly from SVA brings me scraps of fabric she can't use, and I print onto them.

'In 2013 I attended Glastonbury Festival with a group of about ten letterpress printers as part of Glastonbury Free Press. We had the Heidelberg, which is like the Rolls-Royce of printing presses. However, the electrics blew up, so our letterpress posters were handed out instead of the newspaper they'd been planning to print. I'd written something called "Worthy Farm Song". We raised £10,000 for the festival charities over the four days in poster sales, which was such a boost for letter press.

'It's just so wonderful having the café so close to the workshop. I've always been attracted to cafés. I used to run a community book shop in Cornwall, which was next door to the Quasar Coffee House – a mythical café with a pinball machine. They would play their own LPs, mostly rock and roll and blues. It was the end of the sixties, beginning of the seventies, and they served real coffee, which you couldn't get in many places then.'

Visiting Dennis's studio is like walking into another world. Prints line the walls, and there is just room to walk between the bookcases, printing presses and wooden drawers full of different type. All around are works in progress, inks and shelves full of books. His craft is a cool culmination of so many threads of his colourful and diverse life experience, a joining of the love of words, maps and printing, a passion for a life beyond the mundane.

Dennis prints his own work and that of other poets onto handmade cotton recycled rag paper, old Ordnance Survey maps, coloured paper, foil and cloth. Once a year, he attends a big letterpress fair at the village fete in Whittington near Cheltenham, run on the first Saturday in September by John Randle of Whittington Press. John publishes *Matrix* annually, which he describes as 'a work of art' in the world of letterpress, and a thing of great beauty. The hardback publication is available from Whittington Press.

Dennis, who is now in his eighties, still cycles, still works from his workshop most weekdays and does a regular posters and book stall where he sells second-hand and new paperbacks and his own work at the Shambles Market on Saturdays. He can often be found having breakfast in Star Anise Café with his lifelong friend and fellow poet, Jeff Cloves.

Emily Lawlor

MOSAIC ARTIST

~ ChinaJack Mosaics ~

Emily is a self-confessed china obsessive. 'I love the makers' marks, the patterns from companies such as Spode and Burleigh and the rich history and industrial heritage of the Staffordshire potteries.'

Emily grew up with Irish parents who moved to Cirencester when her dad got a job there – Emily was ten at the time. She remembers her mum telling her traditional Irish folk stories, Grimms' and Hans Christian Andersen stories, which she says gave her a sense of magic. As a child she enjoyed building fairy houses, making small things, playing out in the woods, and creative imagination.

Growing up in a family where storytelling and poetry reading together was a big part of family life, it has continued to be a big part of Emily's life. One of her earliest memories is of a pack of felt pens in a cardboard box in the kitchen that her mum had ordered specially from France and which she loved using.

Emily really loved school and worked very hard, concentrating on academic subjects and having a love for history and music. After a gap year, she went to study a degree in archaeology but hated it, so dropped out and changed direction. She did part-time life drawing at Bourneville College of Art and started to put together a portfolio before training as a secretary and travelling in India.

Emily's first secretarial job at the age of 21 was working for the National Trust at their HQ in London as a PA to the ceramics conservator. She toured the properties with her boss, as they 'put the houses to bed' by putting ceramics into storage and learned about traditional stapling methods of fixing broken china. This inspired her, at the age of 24, to do an art foundation at the City and Guilds of London Art School in Kennington with a view to continuing to a degree in ceramics conservation. Having worked, Emily found it a privilege and luxury to be a student after spending a few years in the workplace.

Emily went on to do her degree in public art at Chelsea Art School, specialising in ceramics and mosaics and did secretarial temping work in the summer holidays, working for Penguin Books and a newspaper group. She has always loved the use of text, and stories are a thread which run through her work. She feels very fortunate to have done a degree at a time when grants were available and further education did not mean coming out with a huge debt, giving students the time to immerse themselves in the coursework, which she feels was a real privilege.

After graduating, she got a job working for an art and architecture practice in Free Form Arts in Hackney as a community artist. She worked on projects in hospitals, schools and libraries and was involved in community consultation. She became really interested in arts and health, which is now her speciality.

The practice worked with site-specific artworks and Emily worked on projects including mosaic and brickwork. Emily also worked with an artist she met there, along with a storyteller, on projects with asylum seekers in Dover and the Traveller community in Lewisham, using traditional song and storytelling and facilitating printmaking and photography projects, involving the community participants in the projects. There would often be a book for the project as well as an exhibition, and the participants would often get a book at the end.

'I love the makers'
marks, the patterns ...
and the rich history and
industrial heritage of the
Staffordshire potteries.'

Recording the stories of asylum seekers who often had harrowing tales of travelling by foot across mountains, was such an important process for people who had lost everything. With the refugee and asylum seeker community, telling the story of their journey is so important. There was a lot of laughter and joy working together despite the adversity that people had experienced. These projects were often Lottery and Arts Council funded.

After her daughters were born in 1999 and 2002, Emily brought up her young family while working part time on small art projects and then when her daughters were older, she started working with ArtShape in Gloucester on community arts for mental health and well-being. Latterly, since her children have grown up, she has worked in a local hospice in the art room where laughter is the heart and soul of the artistic process, a very healing and warm experience as part of

the creative process. 'So many people have lost a special part of their week because of the funding cuts in mental health and the arts, I think it's a great loss to the most vulnerable in society.'

'The start of ChinaJack came about when we had this really beautiful Irish hand-painted china that had belonged to my great-great-grandmother, which Mum would always get out of special occasions. One Christmas, Mum had a stack of these beautiful plates and she tripped over, and all the plates smashed, so I had this box of smashed china. I kept saying, "I'm going to make something special with that." Originally, I started making Union Jacks with them and realised I liked working within a grid or a pattern and the idea of the iconic Union Jack with makers' stamps and text.

'For many years, I have done the Quenington Fresh Air Sculpture Show and in 2017 they invited me to make an installation for the wall of the house, so I made a large flock of swallows in flight. At the time, my mum was really ill, and making the birds for the exhibition kept me going in between caring for mum. Mum passed away just before the private view, and as I walked to my car, I saw a beautiful dead swallow by my car. For me birds represent freedom, hope, fairy tales, and this felt like such a special thing as I'd spent all this time making swallows.' Birds also reflect Emily's love of nature and her blue tit designs were inspired by the birds she sees on the feeder outside her garden studio, a wooden cabin which she describes as her sanctuary.

Every piece of china is cut with snippers and carefully sorted into 'potential body parts' in labelled plastic containers to be used for bird eyes, wing tips, makers' marks and blue tit bodies. There are also boxes of different colourways snipped and ready to use. Every last bit of china is sorted into a box so that nothing is wasted.

There are stacks and stacks of old plates. She sources old vintage tableware at charity shops, car boots, auctions and house clearances. Although she has started keeping some of the old ceramics she collects, Emily says she doesn't have any qualms about cutting up the china because a lot of it has come to the end of its domestic life, so this is its very last usage. Often it is cracked, chipped or outdated. 'I love going about looking for china in charity shops, auctions, market stalls and car boot sales, thinking, "that would make a great feather, that would make a great tail feather."'

> 'I love going about looking for china in charity shops, auctions, market stalls and car boot sales, thinking "that would make a great feather, that would make a great tail feather'

Emily has a sketchbook where she draws birds, working from photographs to create the design for the bird outline, which is crucial. Once she is happy with her designs, they are made into templates and cut out of plywood by her husband, who also sands

down the edges for Emily to varnish and prime. She makes batches of around twelve birds 'or a baker's dozen' at a time, placing the snipped ceramic onto the prepared plywood base, before grouting and finishing with a coat of varnish.

She is always working on new designs, which take a while to develop. There is a batch of swallows laid out on the work bench, getting their wings and bodies placed on the bases. Emily says this is her favourite part, choosing colourways and designs of china for finished pieces.

On the worktop a new batch of china is being broken up, ready to be stored for making. Funnily enough, cleaning off the grout is a little bit like archaeology, which is where Emily first started when she left school.

Most of Emily's commissions come through her Instagram and Pinterest accounts, and through the six galleries and shops she has stock in. Her range of swans, blue tits, swallows and love birds are available from the Made in Stroud shop and Brewery Arts, as well as from her website. She also exhibits at the biennial Quenington Fresh Air Sculpture Trail.

'I feel really lucky to be part of the thriving scene in the area. A touch of fairy tale has brought me to this point, a sense of magic and also a celebration of birds. All mixed in with my childhood experiences, stories and beautiful creatures in the Hans Christian Andersen fairy tales such as the swallow in Thumbelina and the Wild Swans.

www.chinajackmosaics.com

Instagram: @chinajackmosaics

Emily McNair

TAILOR

I meet Em in her studio in town. We are surrounded by neatly organised tape measures, button jars and dressmakers' scissors. Bundles of fabric are folded in an old haberdashery cupboard that was gifted to her by a customer. She is gifted tins of buttons and sewing boxes on a regular basis and we are surrounded by the wonderful haberdashery. As Em points out, good studio space is hard to find. Her current place in town is perfect; light and spacious, with a display area for her collections and a massive cutting and making table.

'I teach right-handed,' she explains, 'but I work left-handed.'

She is working on some new designs using vintage silk saris from India, transforming them into boleros, robes, scarves and hair bands. No scrap of fabric is wasted. Love for the planet is at the heart of Em's work – reducing, reusing and recycling, upcycling, careful sourcing and looking for ways to reduce waste and create the smallest environmental impact while creating a high-quality garment.

'I like couture, pin-sharp precision dressmaking for weddings. I love to embroider, although the time-consuming nature of this means that I don't get commissioned to do that much of it. My great-grandmother was an embroideress and worked on stuff that is in the V&A. Apparently, she learned by going into the V&A and asking to see some of their historical Elizabethan pieces. My grandma used to make bobbin lace. She went to trade school from 1935 to 1936 and at home I have all of her sample pieces preserved. Occasionally, I'll get them out and look at them. Hand-sewn buttonholes and tiny pin tucks. Techniques which are all but lost now.

'My earliest sewing memory is embroidering Grandpa's initials onto the corner of handkerchiefs for a birthday present and he died when I was seven, so I must have been five or six. I also remember sitting on Granny's knee and she would operate the pedal of the sewing machine and she had her hands over my hands and would guide garments through the sewing machine.

'I also remember as a child going to Scotland with my other granny and, to entertain me, we made clothes out of paper napkins from the B&B for my dolly. I got into trouble in reception at primary school for showing the kids how to make dolls' shoes out of newspaper in a maths class, "Holding court in the corner," the teacher said.

'One of my grandfathers could sew, my other grandfather was a novelist and a playwright, so I was immersed in creativity as a child. It was just everywhere. I don't ever remember not making things. I grew up with a curiosity, a love of literature, being taught to sew.'

Em loves the idea of passing on skills to the next generation, stuff that school doesn't teach you, cooking, gardening, practical skills.

'Growing up in Stroud, I was very limited with the choice of clothes I could buy because of my size. I was so little there was only one shop I could shop at, BeWise, for the kids' clothing. I really wanted to develop my own style, or more accurately, fit in with everyone else at school. I saved up £50 from paper rounds, birthdays, Christmas and doing odd jobs for people. My stepdad matched this, and I bought my first sewing machine. I was 12.

'At the time, there were some great fabric shops in Stroud. The guy in the shop helped me to choose a pattern, the fabric and the right thread. Actually, it was a complete disaster. I didn't quite buy enough fabric, so when I was laying the pattern out on the fabric, I moved the pieces around. Of course, it being corduroy, I cut one of the trouser legs with the cord going in the

wrong direction. So, I cut the front leg panels in half, patchworked them and made the trousers – which I wore. That's a mistake you only make once.'

Em started helping with costume making for school productions at Archway. 'Towards the end of school, we did a production of *Grease* and I played Sandy, and made my own costume, a yellow gingham circle skirt and blouse.'

After school Em trained as an actor and was living in Bristol. Never managing to make the leap to London, which was where the 'real' work was, she got lots of extra roles but found it tricky juggling 'bread-and-butter' work with acting jobs. Around this time, her flatmate's sister was getting married and Em made the wedding dress. She also made herself a winter coat. Someone stopped her in the street and asked her where she had got it and commissioned one there and then. She was working in a fabric shop at the time and says it had never occurred to her before that moment that it would be possible to make a living from sewing, unless working as a costume director or on film sets. 'By the time I was 18 I had made my first wedding dress, begun working as a jobbing dressmaker and created my first collection. I made clothes for rave culture and sold on early eBay. However, after a couple of years my designs started getting copied and made cheaply and I felt greatly discouraged.'

Having built her label up from home while bringing up children, Em has recently taken on a studio away from home and now juggles being a parent with running a business, doing the school run and being creative. She is also, astonishingly, doing an online creative writing course, writes a blog for her website and is very active on her social media.

Em's work is influenced by a desire to address ethical, sustainable clothing production which is kind to people and to the planet. Although she has always been interested in this, recently she has felt compelled to push the business in this direction. She has experienced a sense of urgency to find better ways of doing things. The fashion industry is estimated to produce 10 per cent of the world's carbon emissions.

Em likes to source sustainable fabrics and deadstock fabrics which have been produced by fashion houses but not used. Historically, this would have been either incinerated or put into landfill but there is now a trend for making it available for sale. In addition, she uses vintage fabrics, loving the concept of things having already been used for what they were intended and now being made into something else. Her sari collection is a great example of this ethos in action. 'Everything about creating sustainability in business is about finding balance, researching, making choices, and holding oneself accountable,' she says.

'I always think that what I do is somewhere in between art and engineering – turning a two dimensional object – fabric – into a three dimensional object – a garment or accessory.'

Although she likes clean lines and understated elegance in her designs, she points out that with vintage fabric you often have to let the fabric speak for itself. So, a much more flexible approach is required. Although 'formally' untrained, she collects coffee-table books and instructional books, and continues to be self-taught, using YouTube tutorials to learn new skills and techniques. She trials new techniques on her own garments and samples, perfecting them before using them on client commissions.

Em loves the variety of her working life. And she loves to challenge herself, from working with customer ideas for a wedding dress to repairing someone's favourite dress, to creating her own capsule collections. 'I always think that what I do is somewhere in between art and engineering: turning a two-dimensional object – fabric – into a three-dimensional object – a garment or accessory.'

One of Em's big projects in the past decade was creating uniforms and accessories for the Brussels Ball at Berkeley Castle, curated and produced by Amaury Blow. As part of this project, she repaired some old film costumes and made ten Gloucester and two Prussian jackets. In total, she sewed on 240 brass buttons by hand.

I asked Em what her most challenging commission was – a wedding dress made in four days! 'The customer contacted me ten days before her wedding. She wasn't happy with the dress she'd had made. I saw her the very next day. We sorted out fabrics, I ordered them the next day. The day after that they arrived, then I made it, getting it ready for a couple of fittings in between. It was a beautiful, simple 1940s-style silk crêpe dress with a silk organza jacket. The customer was really happy. Making someone's wedding dress is always a great honour and something you absolutely have to get right. The whole experience has to be as stress free and smooth as possible for the bride from start to finish, reassuring them and making their special day the best ever.'

www.emilymcnair.com

Email: hello@emilymcnair.com

Fiona McBryde

SOAP MAKER

- *Soap Folk* -

Fiona works from a bright, sunny studio in a rather stunning converted industrial building between Stroud and Nailsworth. Here she makes natural, cold-processed soaps using essential oils and plant-based ingredients. The unit is fully shelved out with racking stocked high with soaps at various stages of production, waiting to cure, or ready to be wrapped. The smell is gorgeous, a heady mix of lavender, rose, lemon and mint, among others. On the scrubbed pine table inside the glazed wall sits a vase of fresh flowers and some homemade cake. There is a Roberts radio in the open-plan kitchen area.

Fiona fell in love with the idea of soap making when visiting Stroud Farmers' Market with her family in 2000. She remembers visiting a stall selling handmade soap and being fascinated, and this stuck with her. She bought a second-hand book on soap making and started experimenting. The recipes in the book suggested using palm oil, which Fiona had never heard of and didn't know where to get, so she substituted for olive or coconut oil, stuff she could find on the supermarket shelves. She immediately found that the soap-making process made it impossible to make just one bar of soap and she would always end up making twelve bars at a time and found herself stockpiling soap, which she would then share with family and friends.

When she had her own children, she really enjoyed having a gentle product to use at home, knowing all the ingredients that had gone into it. Around 2016, Fiona describes herself as being 'at a turning point' in her life. Both her girls were at primary school, and she was wondering which direction to take. She belonged to a village book club and had just read *The Myth of Modern Motherhood*, which she describes as being about how women tend to put their lives on hold for their children – supporting home and school life, worrying about costumes for World Book Day, getting involved in the PTA, with the pressure to 'do it all', with the career being the thing that falls off. Meanwhile, their husbands would be off fulfilling their careers.

Fiona wanted to get back into the workplace but felt her confidence had taken a bit of a dent. In conversation with her friend Susie, who is a fabric designer, she started playing with the idea of starting her own business but had no idea what to do. The turning point came when, in 2017, there was a post on the Made in Stroud shop social media asking for soap makers as the main soap maker in the shop had moved to Cumbria. Fiona saw the post and thought, 'Oh! I make soap!' She emailed the shop, sent off the application and then rang her partner and said, 'Wow! I've just done something really rash!'

Popping to see Susie, Fiona discussed the idea with her. 'I think I can do this. I think this is it. I know how to make soap. Made in Stroud are asking for soap. Can you help me set up? If I'm going to do this, let's make it the best thing that we can possibly do.'

That Christmas she had her first sales in the shop. Susie printed some of her existing designs onto paper to wrap the soap, and Fiona found she absolutely loved the whole process. That New Year, Fiona and Susie sat down to design Soap Folk's own original products, having come up with the name together. They surrounded themselves with all the scents, came up with the butterfly logo (the Adonis Blue, which thrives on the rare grasslands of Rodborough Common), and discussed how the wrapping for each item of the range would look. They decided on riotous bunches of peppermint and undertook the packaging design process together. Susie was also, says Fiona, a great emotional support.

Susie and Fiona have designed a paper for each soap and a collar for the brand, price, batch code and ingredients. Each soap is individually hand wrapped after being hand stamped with the Soap Folk name. All her packaging decisions are made with the environment in mind, to minimise her impact on the planet.

Fiona started making soap at home in the kitchen, which she describes as 'a disaster'. The lye is very caustic with a very high pH, and their wooden handmade worktops are now permanently marked with chemical burns from soap splashes. She then moved into her partner's study at home. At one point she spilled a whole load of peppermint soap all the way down the stairs, staining the carpet, and she says keeping the cat out of the soap-making room was a mission in itself. Fiona thought, 'If I'm really going to do this properly, I'm going to have to move this out of the house and get a workshop!'

Fiona's neighbour, Tom Knowles Jackson, had just taken on the Clay Loft and suggested she take a studio there. She had no background in running a business but found social media a great way to find the right stockists, independent design-focussed retailers who are genuinely interested in the maker.

Fiona explains to me the history of soap making, how all household detergents would have originally been made using 'whatever was in the kitchen', and how the basis for all soaps is an oil or a fat and an alkaline. Traditionally in the UK, the fat would have been tallow, lard or pig fat, which would have

been rendered down by boiling, and the alkaline would have been ash from the fire. This would have made a quite caustic soap that would have been used for everything – laundry, household cleaning, skin washing, hair. Of course, nowadays nobody would want a soap made with pig fat.

By contrast, modern detergents all appear to be quite distinct but are basically the same product with differing amounts of water and various scents. Although the pH in a liquid eco bodywash will be different from an eco laundry product, that will be the only difference. We now use detergents which are 80 per cent water, so even eco products are actually 'not that eco' as we are transporting water around. Also, as soon as water is added, a preservative then needs to be added as bacteria can be introduced. With soap, because it is a solid product, no preservative is needed and there is no water being shipped.

Fiona's process is to mix the fatty acids, essential oils and vegetable oils, with the lye, the very strong alkaline, and getting them to merge. This creates a process called saponification, which converts the oils into glycerine, and creates a new ingredient. She uses coconut butter and shea butter with coconut oil, gently melts them and warms the olive oil, pours in the sodium hydroxide, mixes this up and it generates heat – it's a very environmentally friendly process as very little energy is needed. After stirring for a while, the consistency changes and it turns into a milky soap batter, and essential oils and botanicals are added at this 'thin trace' stage. Some essential oils speed up the process, which is also determined by the time of year and therefore the differing room temperature.

The batter is poured into moulds at a 'heavy trace' consistency. The saponification process continues for around twenty-four hours. The soap is then 95 per cent saponified, the last 5 per cent happening over the next four weeks, during which the soap is curing and the pH changing. Soap will always have a high pH and that is what preserves it.

Choosing the oil blends is something Fiona loves. Her oils are chosen with several criteria: they must be smells she loves, they must be from a sustainable source, and they must be available at a price to make the soaps affordable.

Since starting her enterprise in 2016, Fiona has started making guest soaps, limited edition gift boxes with soap dishes that are from some of her neighbouring potters at The Clayloft, as well as lip balms and bath oils. She sells her offcuts in a paper bag of 'All Sorts', minimising waste and offering great value.

So, what's her top tip for anyone who wants to start their own enterprise?

'Do what you love, do it well, do it in the way that you want, do it at your own pace. I still love making soap. In theory, as the business grows, I can get other people to do the things I don't like doing myself!'

Soap Folk soaps are now to be found on the shelves in more than fifty design-led gift shops all round the UK and on Fiona's website.

www.soapfolk.com
Instagram: @soapfolk
Facebook: soapfolk
Email: fiona@soapfolk.com

Gemma Sangwine

MILLINER

As we talk, Gemma is sitting at her desk surrounded by vintage costume jewellery. One of her trademark activities is making tiaras, hair clips and hair combs using vintage jewellery.

Gemma shares a studio with her sister Victoria and her best friend from college, Nick Ozanne. 'It's part of an old textiles mill and we've been here since 2009. When we were looking for a suitable space we asked everyone we met if they knew of anywhere. At the time, the SVA Open Studios were on, a perfect time for networking, and the artist Maggie Shaw put us in touch with our current landlords.'

Her creations are designed to be comfortable and easy to wear as well as being unique, bespoke and beautiful. Instead of walking down the aisle in a standard headpiece, which is sold alongside their wedding dress, the bride can have something completely unique, a potential future heirloom made with a piece of family jewellery of sentimental value. 'Every single piece I make is different, I don't mass manufacture at all, I love it and my clients love it, and the opportunity for self-expression and originality.'

Gemma's typical customer is either the bride, the mother of the bride or the mother of the groom, who comes to the studio for a consultation three or four months before the event. She enjoys getting to know them, their personality, and understanding the type of wedding being planned. When they come for their final fitting, and to pick up their piece, Gemma says it's lovely seeing how delighted they are with their bespoke item. 'Manufactured tiaras can really

pinch and be uncomfortable, whereas obviously bespoke items fit comfortably and make the bride's day more joyful.'

Gemma has been working with local wedding dress designers, cake makers, florists, stylists, photographers, hair and make-up artists who share similar values around fair trade, handmade and ethical, building up a great portfolio of images to give brides an idea of the range of products she can make and how to achieve a beautiful, eco-conscious wedding that also reflects the couple's style and personality.

She also makes percher-style hats and buys old hats and re-blocks them, all aimed at keeping stuff out of landfill and creating beautiful accessories. 'I look at hats as adornment. We've really got out of the habit of wearing hats. If you look back to the fifties and sixties, everybody wore one, and a woman wouldn't go out of the house without a hat, gloves, handbag and shoes, all matching and co-ordinated. Similarly, hairstyles were much more elaborate, and women knew how to style their hair up and pin a hat into it, which was very much part of their outfit. Nowadays, women often feel quite intimidated by the thought of wearing a hat, so I am very aware of making comfortable, stylish hats which women feel confident wearing and make you stand up tall and feel great. I'm quite sensitive and gentle when I'm fitting hats for my clients and am aware of their body language. I am always happy to go back to the drawing board, if necessary, to make exactly the right hat for the person so they'll feel fabulous wearing it.'

Gemma tries not to use any glue at all in her millinery, hand sewing everything on her hats so they can easily be taken apart and remodelled. Since childhood she has had an aversion to waste and says that she always sees the creative potential in things which are unloved or discarded but can now become part of something new, beautiful and unique. Using something that has potentially come to the end of its life, like a costume necklace with a broken clasp, she takes the diamanté and marcasite and makes it into something else.

After studying art foundation at Croydon College, Gemma went to Winchester School of Art to study textiles and fashion. At this stage, she was not clear whether she was going to become a textiles designer working for a large company, a fashion designer or a maker. After graduating, she and her partner at the time went travelling and when they came back just did 'any job' to save up the money to go travelling again.

Gemma's hobby was sewing and making things and she started making bags and accessories using her lifetime collection of vintage jewellery, clothing and fabrics with

'I have taken part in the Textile Trail and Select Trail open studios over the years, it's a great opportunity to meet people, share knowledge and skills, and get feedback on your designs.'

her mum's sewing machine. In 2001 she took a stall at Covent Garden Market in the Apple Craft Market selling her handbags. Unfortunately, about a month after she started, the Twin Towers catastrophe in New York meant that trade at the busy London market disappeared overnight as the tourist trade ceased.

After her six months travelling and working in South America, Gemma returned to the family home in Surrey for a while, got a part-time job and continued making accessories as a sideline. Her parents were thinking of moving to Gloucestershire and asked if she would like to move here with them. Thinking that the move could bring new creative opportunities, she came to visit Gloucestershire with her parents. She was blown away by the textiles heritage, the International Textiles Festival in Stroud, and the culture of the artisan arts. 'Stroud felt like a really good place to be.'

Having moved to Stroud, Gemma did a variety of temping agency work and got a job locally as a spot painter with Damien Hirst's Science studio in Brimscombe. 'I loved working at Science and being part of a community of artists working together.' However, in 2009, Science was closed because of the recession and she was made redundant. Describing this as a real crossroads in her life, Gemma, who had now split up with her long-term partner, spent some time thinking about how she would like her life to be. She decided Stroud was a nurturing place which could support her as a maker and decided to stay.

Having committed to staying here, Gemma found a couple of part-time jobs and began developing her own work in her free time. She joined the Handmaids collective of creatives started by Tamsin Mallison. They had a stall in the Shambles Market and then at Stroud

Farmers' Market and she really enjoyed both having an outlet and being part of a group of makers, with the encouragement and peer support that went with being part of a creative community.

In 2014, when she was making fabric corsages and hair clips, Gemma decided she'd like to learn more skills and signed up for a three-month millinery course in Cirencester New Brewery Arts, learning millinery one morning a week. About three months later, the course leader advertised a vacancy for an assistant for her studio in Cheltenham. She applied for the job, which she describes as being a bit like an apprenticeship. The course tutor, and now Gemma's employer, was part of a lineage in the millinery world, having been trained by Rose Corey, hat maker to the Queen Mother.

In 2016 Gemma entered the Three Counties Wedding Awards and won the Best Bridal Millinery category, both for Gloucestershire and overall for the three counties. More recently, the independent bridal boutique the White Room in Minchinhampton now stocks her designs where they are displayed alongside dresses from internationally renowned local designer Savannah Miller.

Gemma's studio is lined with antique display cabinets full of found treasures and new creations. 'This is a bit of a hoarder's paradise. I have stuff here that I've had since I was a teenager. I've always bought up little bits of lace, haberdashery, beadwork, fabrics, fabric remnants and anything that catches my eye. I love shopping at charity shops and from Vintage Mary in town. Even if I want a tiny pair of embroidery scissors or a reel of thread, I will go to Vintage Mary and try to buy it second-hand first, so I'm recycling. I love the stall, they have everything there.'

Being a vegetarian and working towards being vegan, Gemma has an ethical buying policy for her feathers. She is switching to naturally shed feathers, so she and her friends and family pick up feathers off the ground during moulting season, which she then cleans and sanitises to remove any dirt and mites. She also buys vintage feathers and second-hand feather trims and accessories, so she always has a variety in stock and doesn't have to resort to buying new. 'I love feathers and I love working with feathers, so that's a way I can carry on working with them without having to buy new. You can cut and reshape a pigeon's feather and make it into something really interesting.'

Gemma often collaborates with other local designers and businesses, including embroiderer Jan Knibbs and colourful printed textiles brand Humphries and Begg. 'I have taken part in the Textile Trail and Select Trail open studios over the years, it's a great opportunity to meet people, share knowledge and skills, and get feedback on your designs. Made in Stroud was my first stockist in the area, I joined in 2011.'

Alongside her making business, Gemma works in a local vintage shop, Strangeness and Charm, and for the Textile Treasury doing repair and restoration work, tiny invisible stitching. This is mainly working with nineteenth- and twentieth-century textiles and she has found herself repairing original William Morris pieces that she has only ever seen in books or museums before, which are a real honour to work on.

www.gemmasangwine.com

Instagram: @gemmasangwine

Liz Dart

STAINED-GLASS ARTIST

Inside the family home, atop a steep hill and surrounded by wooded slopes, Liz Dart is working in her studio accompanied by Dash, the whippet, who is lying in his cosy bed listening to the radio. The sun shines in through the large window, coloured glass lies cut and ready to lead, and pencilled designs are ready on the work bench.

Liz began her long career as a stained-glass artist 'completely by accident', she explains, at the age of 18 when she had just finished her A levels. Having lost interest in her A levels halfway through, she failed her exams 'miserably' so that university wasn't an option. She went to the job centre as she needed a job, and when asked what she was good at replied, 'Art, I'm quite good at art.' The person looked through a little book and said, 'Yes, we have a stained-glass artist in Nailsworth who has just started on an apprentice scheme. You can go there as an apprentice.'

Liz didn't even know what stained glass was apart from something you find in churches. She took the apprenticeship and was able to walk to work from home every day. 'My first day, I was set to work stripping down an old stained-glass panel from South Cerney church. The panel was about four foot wide by about one and a half foot wide, with each piece of glass measuring about an inch. I'd never worked with glass before. I had to remove each piece of glass using a pair of pliers, carefully pull all the old lead off each piece of glass and put each piece of glass on another board in its original pattern to be completely re-leaded. After a week I was completely hooked.'

In her role as an apprentice, Liz often worked on site, climbing up scaffolding in churches all over Gloucestershire. At Gloucester Cathedral, she helped on a broken panel above the choir stalls behind the organ and altar before the High Altar. 'The window was about 80 foot up, and I had to climb up eight stages of scaffolding tower and a ladder at the top. As I'm not great with heights, it took me about half an hour to climb up with all the tools. I'd stop for a break for a few minutes to regain my composure at each level.'

Her job was to replace broken 'quarries', or little diamond-shaped pieces of glass in situ, using a blunt tool to bend the lead back around the edge of the glass, break what was left of the glass to get it out, clear out the channel of the lead, cut a new piece of glass to fit, pop it into the existing lead, bend the lead back and cement the finished work. All up a ladder, 80ft up in the air.

When she came back down the scaffolding, which she describes as worse than going up, 'because you have to look down', there was a priest sitting in the choir stalls. He congratulated her, saying, 'I wasn't sure you were going to make it. I've been praying for you the whole time.' Liz says it obviously worked!

Having gained her City and Guilds qualification and after eighteen months of her apprenticeship, Liz was advised to apply for a foundation course in art and design, as she had learned as much as she could about all the practical aspects of stained glass. She applied and was accepted at Stroud College to do her foundation, then went to uni to do a degree course at Wolverhampton in glass design and sculpture. She says she ought to do more life drawing, but it's finding the time to do it all.

Liz set up her business in March 2000 when she was left some money and bought a kiln and tools so that she could work from her home studio. Around this time, she was working to pay off uni debts and started making her own creations in her spare time, beginning with very simple geometric coloured glass panels, which she sold through a small gallery in Nailsworth. 'My work was a bit of trial and error to begin with.'

Getting a regular stall at the farmers' market gave her the incentive to sit down and design a range that would fit a certain price bracket. Liz says that thinking about what most people would want to spend has helped her to create her range of products over the years, finding a balance between the average budget and what people want to buy, rather than thinking, 'I'll make this and see what people will pay for it'. As she says, 'Some things work and some things don't.' She has regular customers who buy panels to a certain theme, some loving her fish and others her floral representations.

'I'm a lifelong William Morris enthusiast. This is reflected in my work, which is very much influenced by my love of nature and the birds, flowers and wildlife in the garden around the family home.'

Coloured glass sheets are made using metal oxides, and Liz buys her glass wholesale from a supplier. Blues are cobalt, greens are copper, red is iron, yellows are chrome, and dayglo colours are made using slightly radioactive oxides. A bright yellow is made using uranium. The pinks used in mouth-blown antique glass are made with gold and cost twice as much as the other colours.

Liz says her favourite colour is the blue glass, which everyone loves as it's soothing and calming. She was recently commissioned by the NHS to design and make a stained-glass panel for a multifaith 'reflective area' in a local psychiatric hospital. She designed a tree using lots of blues and greens and enjoyed playing with colours and finding the right mood.

There are two main techniques that Liz uses, traditional stained glass with lead and cement, and copper foiling, which is quite a clean version of making. The copper foil is soldered with a 50/50 tin and lead which is run over the surface of the foil. This has been prepared with flux to make the solder stick. The latter technique is used on her very popular greetings cards.

Her painted designs are made using tracing paint, which contains oxides and ground glass powder and is mixed with water and gum Arabic to create a liquid. Liz paints images of wildlife, plants and flowers onto her glass panels, as she is very much influenced by her love of her garden and the view from her studio window, and this is fired at 650 degrees in the kiln until it is vitrified, so the ground glass melts onto the surface of the glass and they become one. When these come out of the kiln, enamels are applied.

Painting is her niche, and her greetings cards and panels are really popular. Her heart panels are popular all year round. 'I'm a lifelong William Morris enthusiast. This is reflected in my work, which is very much influenced by my love of nature and the birds, flowers and wildlife in the garden around the family home. My best sellers are my greetings cards and panels, although I do sometimes work on commissions for window panels and bespoke gifts when I have time.'

Liz's work varies throughout the year. In the spring, she works on building up stock and takes a twice monthly stall at Stroud Farmers' Market, which she first started attending in 2000, having taken some time off to have her two children. She also uses this time of year to take commissions. From August to December, she is making and selling seven days a week, attending shows and markets at the weekends and concentrating on making during the week. She loves attending the farmers' market, meeting people and talking to them. She says that, after working alone, it's so great getting feedback and affirmation. 'The encouragement and enthusiasm, even when customers are not able to make a purchase, are really helpful. Sometimes you have quiet days at markets, but you get paid in compliments.'

Liz's work is available from the Made in Stroud shop, Stroud Farmers' Market and through her social media, Etsy and her own website. She is always happy to receive visitors to the studio by prior appointment.

www.lizdartstainedglass.com

Instagram: lizdartstainedglass
Facebook: @lizdartstainedglass
Etsy: LizDartStainedGlass
Email: lizdartstainedglass@gmail.com

Lizzie Mabley

PRINTMAKER AND FABRIC DESIGNER

Having trained at North Oxfordshire College of Art and Design in art foundation and then textile design, and surface decoration at Brunel University in High Wycombe, Lizzie met her husband, got married and had a family. They moved to Stroud, where they both worked for a local publisher. When she became a full-time mum, she was always doing bits and bobs of making. 'I've always been a sewer, always made my own dresses and clothes. When I was young, I used to make stuff out of paper and scraps of fabric. I used to make clothes for my teddy bears and dolls, made my own clothes, party dresses and ball gowns out of silk. I can't believe it when I see all these expensive prom dresses and I used to make my own. I still love to run up a top or a skirt with lovely fabric.'

Lizzie's business began as My Blue Shed when her children were older and she began working from a shed in the garden, which she decided to clear out and make into a studio, hand printing tea towels and bags to sell at Stroud Farmers' Market and little fairs locally. Originally using block and lino printing, she started screen printing here and still has the original 'I <3 Stroud' screen that she uses for tea towels and cushions sold exclusively through the Made in Stroud shop. During this time, she also embroidered and appliqued cushion commissions. 'They were delightful but extremely time consuming.'

Lizzie had her name down on the waiting list for a studio at Victoria Works, a converted mill building near Chalford. In 2015, she was offered a viewing on the smallest workroom available. She decided that it was time to take that leap of faith and she could cover the rent, allowing her to focus on her craft and make more. After a couple of years, she moved to a studio twice as large in the same building, where her samples of digitally printed fabrics are on display around the walls. Her fabrics are available to buy by the metre, as well as being available as cushions and lampshades made by Lizzie.

As part of the move, Lizzie created her new brand. She looked at the whole ethos and mood of her business and rebranded as Lizzie Mabley Fabric & Home.

'I've always loved fabrics, and I love to see my designs on lengths of fabric; it is really satisfying. When I get my fabric back from the printers and open it up, I love to think that's just my little lino cut. It's fabulous. Really fun. My designs are inspired by nature, plants, flowers, organic shapes, and any patterns I see. I'm very observant and will always take pictures when I'm out. It could be railings, drain covers, tiles. Anything can be taken and made into a design.'

One of the advantages of having a larger studio is that Lizzie can offer one-day workshops where people can design, carve and print in a day and take home something that they've made, from a lampshade to a cushion cover or a tea towel. The workshops are popular, and she particularly loves passing on her skills and seeing participants enjoying creating their own designs. Her main ambition in the classes is to keep the designs simple so that people are happy with their end result.

In the class, the participant's own lino cut is then glued on to a 10cm square wooden block to make it easier to print with. 'I really love to pass on what I know to other people and see them enjoy it. It's an easy and practical thing to do at home. They can go home and start printing their own gift cards and wrapping paper on the kitchen table, it's such a cheap and easy thing to do.'

Lizzie's design process begins as a series of sketches, some of which get transferred by hand with tracing paper onto lino in reverse, then hand carved out with various grades of cutting tools, giving her signature textured and imperfect look. The print then comes out the right way round. She uses a range of sizes of carving tools. 'The thing about lino cuts is that you can see the lines from the carving, and you can see the energy of the design, or you can cut the designs out completely to create a cleaner print.'

The lino cut is printed on to paper or fabric. There are different processes, dictated by the material. If you're printing onto paper, you squeeze the ink onto glass and roller it out, then roll it onto the lino and place the paper on top and press it. Printing paper is more absorbent than drawing paper. Fabric is much more absorbent than paper, making it more forgiving, so specialist fabric ink can be sponged onto the lino, which is then used like an Indian block print.

'It's really nice to see my fabrics in different applications. A design looks so different on a lampshade or a cushion to a seat covering for a dining chair. I suppose that's what I like about fabric, it's really versatile.' Lizzie's sketchbook is brimming with new designs waiting to be used, her biggest dilemma being that she has so many design ideas, but to be commercial she must hone it down to a few designs in collections of colourways to make them easier to market. Usually, each collection has a couple of colourways.

Most of Lizzie's designs are named after family members and favourite garden flowers, giving a very personal touch to her collections. Once she has done a mood board with colour chips, she has a meeting with her digital designer, a friend, to discuss her ideas before getting the design 'Photoshopped' into a repeat print. This is sent off to be printed digitally in England, a waste-free and eco-friendly process that doesn't use any water. 'For me, digital is the way forward as I don't have space to print lengths of fabric here.'

Lizzie still hand prints many of her popular original designs and does all her own sewing, including the piping on her cushions. She also does a bit of upholstery, having attended a one-day course downstairs in the building with Katarina. She loves the versatility of fabric, and

the way that the same design looks so different on a seating cushion or a window blind, for example. She makes all her own lampshades as well as teaching lampshade making and offering lampshade printing workshops.

Lizzie's best-selling items are cosmetic bags, which are popular gifts, hand screen-printed tea towels and small cushions with her bees and crabs on. Moving to digital printing means that she can supply any length of curtain and blind fabric to match her cushions and lampshades. Her metre lengths of fabric samples look like beautiful panels on the wall, in spring colours with a little hint of summer.

Lizzie continues to print her smaller items in the studio and takes part in Open Studios events throughout the year. Her customers really appreciate the unique nature of her designs and enjoy getting to know the artist and seeing the work and skill that goes into making their home furnishings.

Another part of the business is working on design commissions for one-off pieces. One such commission was a funky black spectacle design on red linen for a chaise in the reception area of an independent opticians, which is so quirky and unique. 'The great thing about commissions is that they put you out of your comfort zone. The more you struggle with it, the better the result will be. If there is an element of fear and struggle, then I think that's a good thing. When they come to fruition it's so nice to see the client is happy and the brief has been fulfilled, it's very satisfying.'

Lizzie usually works most days on her business, either on production in the studio or at home on marketing and online sales, balancing the stock levels with the sales. She really enjoys being part of a creative hub and 'going out to work' after being home-based for so long. She enjoys the freedom and discipline of being self-employed, being able to go for walks with friends, teaching, open studios and being able to leave everything out in the studio at the end of the working day, not having to put everything away.

Her own home is full of her own designs: lampshades, curtains, blinds, cushions. 'I try not to bring too much stuff back as I don't want it to be like a Lizzie showroom, but inevitably I do have some of my fabrics at home, because I like them!'

Lizzie takes part in Open Studios each year and sells through the Made in Stroud shop, and customers often find her through her Pinterest account, Folksy and Etsy shops.

www.lizziemabley.co.uk

Instagram: @lizziemableyfabrics
Email: lizzie@lizziemabley.co.uk

Lyndsay Grant-Muller

CYANOTYPE PRINTER

Lyndsay grew up in Bradford as part of a colourful multicultural community, celebrating festivals as well as being around creativity at home. 'I had a lot of time with my mother, who is very naturally talented, doing things like batik, silkscreen printing and papermaking at home. When I was eleven, I made my own silk batik waistcoat with my mum for dress-down day. Mum was always knitting on her knitting machine.'

Their home was full of bright-coloured walls, ridiculous numbers of houseplants and homemade macramé. She cites her mum as very much being her inspiration for her creativity. 'I got a love of plants and nature from my mum.'

Being dyslexic, Lyndsay would spend a lot of time illustrating her textbooks with illuminations. She did have areas of interest, being fascinated with RE and learning about different cultures, symbols and motifs – the importance of geometric imagery in Islam, for example.

Lyndsay left school and did A level art, but finding the limits of the syllabus frustrating, she joined an evening life-drawing class in the local adult education college as a balance to retaking her maths GCSE at age 17, which she needed to be able to teach.

At the Bradford and Ilkley Community College art foundation course Lyndsey found herself immersed in an exciting new culture of street art, skaters and graffiti artists. She experienced her first ever visit to London and worked with really cutting-edge tutors at the time. 'Art foundation was a really exciting time for me and opened up my whole world.'

Lyndsay specialised in photography and was interested in moving image work. 'We were lucky to have a lot of established artists teaching us, it was a really good opportunity to meet people.'

Lyndsay was accepted into Nottingham Trent University to do a photography degree and in the second year took part in an exchange to Long Beach, California, for a semester. 'The main thing for me about being in California was the light. It took me ages to shake off the need to be out taking photographs and to get used to the fact that it was sunny every day.'

Here, Lyndsay found herself experiencing a different lifestyle from the one in Bradford. The education was very different to the UK system; it was very intense. It was 2001, and there were lots of underground parties. Lyndsay found that being around creative musicians and meeting at secret locations like parking lots, and the never-ending summer weather and great light were an exciting experience.

Lyndsay shared a dorm with a girl who owned a car and would take her to parties and on road trips. Her roommate's family lived in Humboldt in the Redwoods, northern California, in a self-built house with land where they grew crops and kept llamas. 'It was like another world. A lot of the hippies had moved from San Francisco to settle there.' She found the whole experience really enriching and inspiring, such a contrast to being brought up in Bradford, where although there was an alternative scene which she grew up around, it was not as wild and free as California.

Returning to complete her degree in photography, she did her final show on an installation based on the work of Eadweard Muybridge and his study of motion, which was a pre-emptor to stop-frame photography. Lyndsay loved the concept that not all movement could be captured in one frame and did a study of sequences of people dancing – a study of improvised dance. She got her friends to come and dance in her bedroom and filmed them with strobe light, editing it together to a rather ethereal piece of music by Aphex Twin. A friend of hers knew the person who owned The Bomb nightclub in Nottingham and Lyndsay's show was put on as an installation in the basement in an igloo-shaped space with a massive sound system, something that she really got a sense of accomplishment from.

After completing her degree, Lyndsay juggled temporary jobs with further study in the film industry, attending an introduction course covering editing, scriptwriting and camera use. She moved to Manchester and joined a VJ crew as an intern, doing visuals in nightclubs, which she loved although she didn't enjoy having to do awful temp jobs alongside it. I ended up just surviving in Manchester with a lot of debt. It was hard to break into the media world there.'

'After uni I just didn't know where to go with my work.' After doing some voluntary work in community video and having built up a lot of experience in the voluntary sector, Lyndsay found out about the European Voluntary Service programme and went to Slovenia, working with photography and video workshops with Roma families who'd escaped the war in Kosovo and Serbia and were living in temporary housing space for refugees.

In Krsko, Lyndsay worked in a youth project making videos with the Roma children about their cultural heritage. She also worked in Ljubljana, the capital of Slovenia, in a village of homes made entirely from corrugated iron. Here, she did darkroom work, developing photographs with young

people and volunteers from the village. There was an end-of-project exhibition which, she says, was probably the shortest exhibition ever as the children loved the photographs so much that they each took their pictures home. All the photographers also donated their cameras to the community so the project could continue after they'd left.

On returning to the UK, Lyndsay successfully applied for a grant with the Community Service Volunteers in Suffolk, working with youth housing organisations and running a project working with young people, teaching them to make a video CV to hand over to employers before the days of YouTube. She also worked in a happiness café for a while as a volunteer, where she ran drop-in workshops in paper making and light sculptures with leaves – creative practice and mental health together demonstrating the value of having company, learning new skills and creating something beautiful.

There was a general shift in culture in 2008 when arts funding dried up, so Lyndsay decided to get into teaching. She really wanted to get her own studio and loved the idea of having a balance between teaching, studio practice and visiting exhibitions.

She eventually moved to Stroud with her partner, looking for a teaching role and not knowing anything about the area. 'My partner said to me, "This place looks quite interesting, shall we see how we get on here?"'

Getting work teaching photography at Stroud College, Lyndsay was finally able to realise her dream of creating her own practice and really got into working with Cyanotype, a process developed by scientist and astronomer Sir John Herschel and taken up by Anna Atkins, a botanist, who is regarded as one of the first female photographers and was one of the first people to publish a book illustrated with photographs.

Considering her work to be 'active mindfulness', Lyndsay loves collecting leaves and flowers to use in her prints and thinks of her work as very much a homage to Anna Atkins. When the chemicals are combined in the correct way, they become sensitive to light. When applied to leaves and then exposed to daylight, a deep Prussian Blue image of the subject emerges on the paper.

Lyndsay keeps a sketchbook where she notes the time of year, strength of the sun and amount of time the print was in the light. She loves the varying resulting shades of blue and the imperfection and experimental nature of the work, especially enjoying seeing things more closely and looking at their structure. She also enjoys collecting things and studying things that she intends to print. 'I was naturally drawn to the process as I have a real passion for blue.'

Working around her planning and teaching, Lyndsay uses her living-room window to make prints, which she carefully frames or makes into greetings cards and mounted prints. (She and her partner live in what used to be an old animation studio where *Animal Farm* was created.) She also teaches this technique at Stroud College to the photography students.

'The process of bringing my work to the public I find quite intimidating.' Lyndsay describes showing her work as 'thrilling but also feeling naked'. She has attended a few markets in Stroud and sells through the Made in Stroud shop.

www.cyanotypeprints.com

Instagram: @lyndsaygrantmuller

Mandy Holder Charles

MAKER OF NATURAL CANDLES AND SOAPS

Having grown up in between London and Gloucestershire, Mandy moved to Cheltenham at the age of 9 to live with her Gran and Gramps. There she spent many happy summers with her cousins, who are like siblings to her. 'I was the typical sixties love child, Mum worked as a model and later for Chanel and as a make-up artist, Dad was a drummer. They were the stereotypical rock 'n' roll couple. I was always dressed to the nines in a Biba dress and hat, whatever the occasion.'

Mandy's grandparents lived in a corner house with a large plot, which was divided in two – the garden, where the children were allowed to play, and the orchard, divided by a fence and with a gate through which the children were forbidden to pass. In the orchard their Gramps had a massive pear tree, plum trees, his vegetable allotment, where he would grow 'everything' and his flower patch, where he grew his beloved freesias among the sweet peas. The only time the kids were allowed in was after the sun had gone down in the summer to water, when they would have hours of fun soaking each other with the hose while watering rows of carrots, broad beans, peas, mint, cabbages, lettuces, runner beans, the rhubarb patch and the herb garden.

After work, Gramps would spend all his free time taking care of his plot. 'I remember the whole patch by the smells of ripe fruit, mint, lavender and roses.'

As rules are made for breaking, Mandy and her cousins would often sneak into the orchard alone. One day, which makes them laugh even to this day, her cousins put her up into the pear tree and she was unable to get down. When their Gramps caught them 'trespassing', her cousins ran away, and she remained stuck in the tree. Her Gramps got a ladder out to try and rescue her, and while he was below, she accidentally moved a branch. The pears were all beautiful and ripe, and a massive piece of fruit fell on her Gramps' head, breaking in half and cutting him as it did so. The kids were 'in the doghouse' until their late-summer bedtime that day. The family still laugh about it to this day.

In the summer, the whole extended family would sometimes go camping to Bream Sands and Weymouth, where Mandy's cousins would bury her in the sand and then run away and leave her, as she was always telling tales, being the youngest. Her memories from this time in her childhood are of the wonderful smells coming from her Gran's kitchen, the smells of the beach, flowers and fresh produce in the garden.

Her Gran would cook and conserve all the orchard fruits every autumn and make crumbles, jams and pies.

In the winter, the kids would sit down at the kitchen table, making pomanders for Christmas from oranges with cloves in, which would be dried all around the house on the radiators ready to have ribbons tied on for gifts and decorations.

Mandy remembers her childhood fondly and her grandparents as always having time for her and being there for her. Her dad is her hero, and she used to go to his rehearsals at his friend John Beckenham's music shop, where she would hang out upstairs with his son, Simon Pegg, who later became a writer and actor. Mandy's dad would often be away playing and used to gig on the riverboats in London, often playing with Joe Loss and his orchestra. Mandy spent a fair bit of time going to gigs and band practice with her dad, which she loved.

> 'All of my candle blends represent happy childhood memories, because memories are so personal, and because smells evoke emotions and happy feelings'

Later on, Mandy's dad and his wife lived in Minsterworth by the river, in a house which often flooded when there was a bore (the tidal wave which travels along the River Severn at high tide and full moon). It was a party house and would often be full of people who would stay up all night drinking, and it was not unheard of for her dad to get the boat out and take everyone out onto the river at 6 a.m. (it's a wonder nobody drowned, the Severn is so dangerous).

In spring, Mandy and her dad would go elvering together, catching the baby eels in fine nets as they migrated upstream. They would take their catch along the road to be weighed, where they would get cash from Willie, who bought all the elvers to sell on to market. She would get half the cash for helping, although she hated scraping them out of the bucket as they were all squirmy. They used to traipse through the mud in Minsterworth to the bluebell woods together and the smell of the flowers reminds her of their time together, as their woodland walks were their only alone and quality time. Although it was muddy, Mandy would inevitably be in her best dress, traipsing through the mud with her dad.

The house at Minsterworth flooded so often that there was a caravan in the garden for when the ground floor was under water, which Mandy found really funny, although her stepmum wasn't so keen on having a completely flooded kitchen.

Mandy had a career in Stroud as a commercial manager for a local paper and left in a state of burnout after fifteen years of working in advertising for the newspaper group. As a teenager, she was really into nice smells and has always had a good nose, so in 2016 she started making candles from home in Amberley, supplemented by part-time cleaning jobs.

Mandy loved candles but was fed up with the smoky and toxic products available on the market. She did loads of research on oils, waxes and wicks and eventually, after a lot of testing, came up with rapeseed wax, for its sustainability and non-toxicity. She really wanted something which would be pleasant and safe to burn in the home. At the time, rapeseed wax was hardly used, and it seemed appropriate as crop that is grown here in the UK and has multiple uses, from animal feed to food oil, as well as being safe to burn when made into a wax.

'Everyone told me the candle market was completely saturated and I was wasting my time, and I got only discouragement. For anyone starting up, I'd say to follow your passion and never give up.' Mandy started making candles and giving them to friends and family and asking for feedback.

The biggest learning curve has been the blending and getting the wax to accept the oils. There are so many blends and scents available, Mandy gave some thought to her range, and decided to use memories as her theme. Mandy started to think about what triggers her happy place and what makes her happy.

Her first blend was plum and rhubarb, which reminded her of her Nan's kitchen, and cooking at the table and preparing lovely food. Pear and freesia reminds her of her Gramps and the hilarious time in the orchard with her cousins. The orange spice reminds her of family Christmases. Lavender reminds her of her childhood and of the present, where she has the plant growing in the garden and where all the neighbours bring bunches from their garden and leave boxes of beautiful cut lavender by her gate to infuse for her candles. In return, she gives them a candle each. A local organic gardener also started collecting herbs from her customers so that Mandy has bay and other herbs hanging from the kitchen ceiling drying to be infused for the candles. She also has a rose garden and dries the rose petals. All the dried petals and leaves end up being kept in airtight glass jars ready to infuse.

The driftwood and rock salt remind her of her happy childhood camping holidays by the coast. The bluebell reminds her of visiting the bluebell woods with her dad as a young girl, a rare time together with just the two of them. 'All of my candle blends represent happy childhood memories, because memories are so personal, and because smells evoke emotions and happy feelings.'

While evolving her product line, Mandy got into yoga classes online and developed the frankincense candle to burn while practising. She also recently began soap making, attending online courses and learning everything she can about how to make soap.

On a camping holiday, Mandy was inspired by the story of women using pebbles to exfoliate their skin in the Lake District, and by the sheep's wool on the barbed wire fencing from the local Herdwick flocks. She started experimenting with wrapping the soap in wool and developed a teen soap containing rosemary and clay in a felted, natural exfoliating 'pebble', which is compostable after use and can be used for mulching once the soap is all used up. There are no microplastics going into the water course during use, unlike the plastic, scrubby sponges sold in high-street chains. Being natural and biodegradable, they are also popular with wild swimmers and wild campers.

She has also developed a rose and wild geranium soap as well as calendula, both also wrapped in natural felt. She is currently working on a range of lip balms and has started creating a range of pamper and self-care boxes.

A year on from planning to expand her business, Mandy has been able to give up her cleaning jobs, which were bad for her back, and focus on her making. She likes her products to be clean, fresh and minimal. So, her candles are not boxed, she offers refills, and packaging is always kept to a minimum. The focus is on high-quality ingredients and good products which are kind to the users and kind to the planet. 'I think everyone has memories of the beach, or their quiet place, or their grandmothers, their aunties or someone special who they really want to remember, and these are the happy places I like to create with my candles.'

Mandy's products are available from the Made in Stroud shop, her website and Etsy.

www.candleco.net

Instagram: @candlecocandles
Facebook: candlecocandles
Etsy: www.etsy.com/shop/candlecobymandy
Email: candleco@mail.com

Maeve With Love

ARTIST

Maeve works from a bright, minimalist new-build studio in Rodborough. She uses a lot of black lines which reflect her love of illustration, graffiti and Art Nouveau, old movie posters and book covers. 'I've always loved things which are a bit kitsch, a bit tongue in cheek, and slightly "naff". I'm also a massive fan of Grayson Perry.'

We are surrounded by portraits, signage and a rack of Maeve's signature t-shirt designs. Her work is influenced by advertising and she uses positive statements and affirmations to create a positive energy. 'It's taken me years to take myself seriously and to refer to myself as an artist. When I graduated, I felt it was impossible to make a living working as an artist and felt I had no idea where to start. I felt I wasn't good enough.'

Sitting in her studio and being surrounded by her work, I feel inspired by Maeve's sprit of never giving up and always finding a way, and find myself wanting to wear her work, so bold, empowering and current and very desirable.

Accessibility of art is a passion of Maeve's, and she finds it sad that people will buy art from superstores because they don't know where to find original artwork, or they don't feel as comfortable in an art gallery.

Describing herself as a typical west London girl, Maeve grew up in Ealing. She loved school and excelled, so much so that she was moved up a year. Maeve has always been really motivated and into art and fashion. Even at the age of 13, she was saving up her dinner money and bus money and would walk forty-five minutes to school and back every day in all weathers so she could buy herself a new outfit for the school disco. 'When I was fifteen, I worked all through the summer holidays so I could give up my Saturday job and attend life-drawing classes on Saturdays.'

'My ambition was always to be an art teacher or art therapist, because I wanted to help people more than I wanted to become an 'artist''

After doing A-level art, Maeve joined a foundation course around the corner from her Nan in west London. She really enjoyed the course, where she was delighted to get the opportunity to do sculpture, life drawing and work with glass. 'My ambition was always to be an art teacher or art therapist, because I wanted to help people more than I wanted to become an artist.'

At uni in Cardiff studying fine art, Maeve had her confidence really knocked by the culture. She found the education very conceptual and pretentious. Memorably, one of the tutors asked her in a crit. session on a photography project, 'What class are you from?' At the time she was young and, describing her family as in many ways 'quite mixed', she didn't have a reply. She didn't want to be coerced into saying her work was a comment on social class when it wasn't.

Maeve found the emphasis on conceptual art over skill in painting and drawing frustrating. As an act of rebellion, she deliberately created work that was a bit kitsch, pretty and tongue in cheek in response to having to deal with a lot of criticism and judgement around her choice of work. She found the emphasis on concepts over skills demoralising and discouraging. She became determined not to follow the crowd just to get A grades and create what would be meaningless work to her. Sadly, the last thing she wanted to do after leaving university in 2003 was to be an artist, and she didn't do any drawing or painting for years.

She was unable to find work after her degree and found herself working in data entry and doing bar work in the evenings. Finding life endlessly mundane and not having any creative outlet, she felt overstretched and uninspired. She had done a few internships but obviously had to earn money so gave them up.

After visiting someone for advice in 2006 because she wasn't sure in which direction to take her life, Maeve became inspired to work in costume design, something she had never considered as a career choice. She retrained, learning technical skills that could be applied in the workplace, meaning she would always be able to earn money doing what she loved.

She enrolled on a course in theatre costume in Edinburgh, where she volunteered for one day a week working for a tailor. On the course she learned to make patterns, cut and construct, and the history of fashion – technical skills rather than design. While in Edinburgh, she found work in costume at the Fringe, working on three events. She also worked on London Fashion Week.

Moving back to London, Maeve visited every theatre, handing out her CV, and got a job working on *Guys and Dolls* starring Patrick Swayze. She loved it immediately, starting out as a dresser and working her way up to deputy wardrobe mistress. She felt completely at home in the theatre, working with fun, colourful, creative people. Feeling that she had 'found herself' at last, while working in a creative environment, she felt inspired to start painting again. She would go home and paint after work, sometimes until three or four in the morning. With this, came an instinctive feeling to pursue

the path of being an artist. After working on some big shows, her confidence had grown and she then started to feel anything was possible.

In 2008 after quitting the theatre, the recession hit, and she was forced to take up admin work and felt miserable working as a receptionist in a film studio. Feeling trapped, she painted the picture 'Hope'. After years of unfulfilling jobs which didn't pay enough money to get by, working evening bar jobs and painting every weekend, Maeve found herself with no cheerleaders in her world. She found herself being criticised for putting text into her work. She was still experimenting with her work and didn't feel it fitted into a gallery setting. She felt isolated in her art and wasn't part of a community. She moved back up to Edinburgh to try and make the art work and had some success in finding stockists for her greetings cards.

Moving back to London again, Maeve got a great job working for a furniture recycling charity and trained to manage teams, opened up new shops and was required to learn to use social media. With improved self-confidence because of her new work, Maeve started using Instagram for the charity and discovered there was a massive women's self-empowerment movement and that her work had become really current. Having been told by people for years that she was losing 50 per cent of her audience by only painting women, she was really encouraged to pursue her passion.

Maeve's reason for using text was, and is, to reflect the self-empowerment movement and as an artist she wanted to do something positive to create that positive energy in return. She had a yoga holiday booked and was looking at active wear. She found it was all plain and rather sporty and decided to print some of her own images onto her clothing. Friends asked if they could buy her work and it was at this point that Maeve realised how she could make her art into a commercial venture. She also wondered whether, if her work became recognisable through her clothing, she could sell her paintings.

Having friends in Stroud, Maeve had been visiting the area for years. They were forever saying that she should move here and would fit right in. As London had become such an expensive place to live, she decided to move to get a bit of space and concentrate on her creativity. It wasn't until she got here that she realised there is a big arts scene and community here.

Being part of a smaller community feels much more supportive than being in a city. When Maeve had a pop-up shop in Lansdown, she really enjoyed the interaction and felt so much more confident. Passers-by would stop off to check out her latest portraits and give her the thumbs up, which was such a contrast to London life, unless it's somewhere like Hackney, which has become prohibitively expensive. She also loves the proximity of everything in Stroud, the lack of rush-hour traffic and the lack of hustle and everyday aggression.

Maeve has always wanted to make artwork that is accessible, not intimidating and available to everyone, whether it's a greetings card, print, t-shirt or painting. After watching the Stacey Dooley series on the fast fashion industry, she paused production while she did loads of research and sourced Fairtrade organic cotton tees. She has also started printing onto preloved and vintage clothing. This is her real passion as she is concerned about the environment and would like to have a positive impact with her creations. Having had experience of working in charity shops, she was aware of the shocking amount of waste from fast fashion going into landfill, not even good enough for rags after a couple of uses.

I wouldn't choose to be an artist, it's not an easy way to make a living, but there's this thing which tells me to just keep going. I used to sit at my desk when I was a receptionist, thinking, "How am I ever going to be an artist?" Social media has transformed things. I am determined to keep going as I have come through so much struggle to get where I am, it just feels like my destiny.'

Maeve's work is available from several independent boutiques and John Lewis pop-ups and she is looking to sell at festivals and markets with her new upcycled range of clothing.

www.maevewithlove.com

Instagram: @maevewithloveart

Melvyn Warren-Smith

ARTIST

Melvyn is a very successful artist based in Stroud town centre. Painting from his front room, which smells sweetly of turpentine and echoes with the sound of good music, there is always coffee on and there are always homemade cakes baked by Marie, his wife. The window out onto the street is a temporary showcase for paintings before they sell.

Melvyn's talent as an artist was first spotted by his head teacher in his last year of primary school, when he was invited to attend Saturday morning art club in Kingston Art School, a bus trip away from home. Sometimes, he would pretend to have missed the bus, preferring to play bow and arrows in the park with his friends. Melvyn remembers the tutors, Mr Mapp, and Mr Murphy who drove a huge Bentley. In fact, the whole experience seemed larger than life in his 10-year-old mind.

To get to the studios, Melvyn had to walk from the bus stop around the corner to the enormous Victorian building up the large sweeping staircase which had a massive cage full of hummingbirds at the top. Even at that young age, he remembers being immediately struck by the life paintings, graphics and colours, coming from working-class post-war East Molesey. 'The whole experience and this world within worlds of the art studios completely blew my mind.'

In 1964, at the height of the sixties explosion of culture, 16-year-old Melvyn got into Epsom Art School to do a foundation course, where he met friends with whom he'd be in bands, make art and hang out. However, Epsom Art School brought in a requirement for five GCEs and he and his friends, who didn't have any qualifications, were moved to Guildford Art School, where they were accepted on talent, not certificates, and continued to study for three years.

Melvyn is full of rock 'n' roll stories of his youth, his musical influences and college days. He played me a recording of him in a jug band in 1965 at Epsom Art School which a friend made on a reel-to-reel tape recorder. Because his friend wasn't happy with the quality, he didn't share the recording for forty years until he converted it to digital and emailed it to the former band members. 'My friend, Top Topham, started the Yardbirds, aged 15, but his father wouldn't let him go on the road as he was too young, so Eric Clapton go the job. Duster Bennett, who tragically crashed on his way home from a gig when he fell asleep at the wheel, leaving a young family. These are the people who influenced me musically.'

At 19, Melvyn was awarded a David Murray Landscape Scholarship from the Royal Academy and was paid to paint all that summer. He also worked at Knoll House Hotel with his friends and went on to live in St Ives for two seasons, getting involved in the art scene there. He couldn't go on to study at the Royal Academy or the Royal College of Art without qualifications.

Melvyn moved to Warwickshire with his first wife, opening a trendy clothing boutique, and worked for a fabulous company which had several shops. Working their way through the recession, it was very successful, but then increasing rent levels, power cuts due to the 'three-day week' and the inevitable theft that goes with having no lighting – and in a time of 25 per cent inflation – meant that the business closed.

That winter, with his first baby on the way, Melvyn went to London to find work. It was snowing and the black cab Melvyn was in slid into another car and crashed. He jumped out of the cab and went for a meeting with the biggest illustration agency at the time, in Windmill Street by Piccadilly. He had a meeting with the boss there, who was in wellies. He rejected Melvyn's work as he specialised in landscapes. Melvyn felt quite despondent and went tearfully to the receptionist, who suggested visiting IPC Magazines.

This he did, and they said to go to another agency, Grestock & Marsh, who specialised in illustrating short stories and serials in magazines. The feedback was the same – Melvyn would need to put figures into his landscapes.

'Always work in a way that makes you excited, and someone will want to buy it. Intuition is more powerful than working for money. In fact following your passion means the money has to follow.'

127

He totally took this on board. He began working with models and hiring costumes and completed his first commission. This was accepted and he got further commissions, ending up with a forty-five-year career as an illustrator, being responsible for hundreds of book covers.

Melvyn got a large commission for a company owned by Robert Maxwell, which he completed and handed in, but never got paid. This resulted in him becoming bankrupt and losing his house. But he did not give up. Having been brought up being told to get a proper job by his dear mum and by society as a whole, he was used to having to fight to be an artist.

In the days before digital, when Melvyn used to get commissions to illustrate novels he would read the novel to get to know the characters and landscapes, divide the novel into twelve illustrated sections, and begin to shoot photos onto film. He had his own photographer, who would light the models. He hired costumes from Angels in Shaftesbury Avenue, and hired a studio. He would then paint from the photographs, working quickly to keep to deadlines.

A lot of Melvyn's work came from Scandinavia. As with all creative industries, he was only as good as his last job, so he worked like crazy, being the director of photography, choosing shots from contact sheets and painting all hours, creating two illustrations a week and often drying the oils using the radiator.

It was around this time that Melvyn got a commission to illustrate Edwina Currie's novel *She's Leaving Home*. He also decided it was time to go it alone in the art world. From the outside, his life was falling apart – no agent, marriage not going well, divorce on the cards.

Melvyn had attended some Tony Robbins events and, deciding to adopt some new approaches to life, he started again. Working independently of his agent and getting great feedback for the job, he grew in confidence. He learned how to market himself and manage his finances, adopting a new life habit that was more congruent with success. He was in control of his own work and cash flow – and he discovered his agent had been sitting on payments for months unnecessarily.

Melvyn had noticed that in the USA, illustrators had a much higher profile and were recognised for their work. So, he got himself invited to the book launch, which was a sixties-themed event on a party boat under Waterloo Bridge. It was a glittering event with 200 guests, including the national press, and Melvyn was called up to make the presentation to the author of the original painting of the cover, which the publishers had bought. This bold move turned his career around completely. He went from being an illustrator working hand to mouth to being a successful artist painting what he wanted to and selling his work.

Using the painting techniques he'd learned in illustration, Melvyn launched himself into developing his work as an artist. As he points out, with his background and education, he had the choice of working in a factory or pursuing a career as an artist – his passion.

His life and work philosophy is to follow your gut. 'Always work in a way that makes you excited, and someone will want to buy it. Intuition is more powerful than working for money. In fact, following your passion means the money has to follow.' He is not afraid of success, but nor does he crave it. He talks about life as going up to the top of a tree, 'If you get distracted by branches you will not get to the top of the tree before it is your time to leave – you won't achieve your potential if you get distracted.'

A typical day for Melvyn starts early with a walk along the canal or river to explore and take photographs of nature and wildlife, getting inspiration for new work. 'Stroud is like a beautifully lit stage set full of wonderful characters just waiting to be recorded in paints.'

He paints every day for many hours and produces an enormous amount of work, sticking to his conviction that if he paints the subjects that he loves, the customers will come. And they do. 'I've always had an innate ability to mix colours,' explains Melvyn, a fact borne out in my experience of attending painting classes with him. His ability to recreate flesh in oils is quite extraordinary.

Melvyn is a shining example of consistency – showing up, working through the fear of success and the fear of failure, which he says is a great motivator. 'Not getting distracted from your life mission is the secret to success. You have to be hungry to push yourself to your potential.'

His work is available to view online and at his home studio as well as on the Saatchi site. His home is open for Stroud Open Studios and by appointment to view his work.

www.melvyn-warren-smith.co.uk

Instagram: @melvynwarrensmith
Facebook: melvyn.warrensmith
Email: melvyn@melvyn-warren-smith.com

Milligan Beaumont

FINE ART TEXTILE AND FASHION DESIGNER

Milligan's sunny studio in the centre of town at the Stroud Valleys Artspace is a room of wonder and imagination. The walls are lined with hand-drawn illustrations of fashion designs, cartoon drawings, embellished fabric samples and magazine clippings of celebs such as Helena Bonham Carter and Grayson Perry wearing her creations. Dried wildflowers, crystals and diamanté butterflies dangle from the ceiling, making tiny sparkly specks shower the studio. On another wall hangs a huge painting by Nettle Grellier, a fellow Stroud artist and friend.

When I first came across Milligan, she was in the Prince Albert, her favourite local pub, wearing a skirt and crop top made from a 1950s red tablecloth and napkin adorned with embroidered black poodles. 'Every Monday morning, I visit Vintage Mary's stall at the Shambles Market, digging for old special fabrics. Most things I find, even doilies, napkins, tablecloths … I just want to wear. I drape them around and fasten with a safety pin. I once made a Westwood-inspired skirt from a load of school tea towels, all black and white – the ones the kids draw their faces on!'

Milligan's artistic style is heavily influenced by traditional Japanese art, particularly old woodblock prints. 'I'm obsessed with the candy-coloured landscapes by Kawase Hasui. The use of colour and composition is divine. I wish I could jump inside! I also love the cheeky but cute Yōkai illustrations from Kawanabe Kyosai; they kind of have an Ed Roth Ratfink vibe! He's another of my most favourite artists.'

> 'I'm obsessed with the candy coloured landscapes by Kawase Hasui. The use of colour and composition is divine... I wish I could jump inside!'

Having never visited Japan, Milligan's utopian vision of the country began as a child watching Studio Ghibli movies and being totally obsessed with Sanrio stationery and Hello Kitty! plush toys. In her teenage years she discovered the colourful prints of Japanese fashion designers such as Issey Miyake and Kansai Yamamoto.

As we chat in her studio, she is hand stitching a jacket of vibrant purple slubbed silk with a shocking pink lining. It is a new design, inspired and drafted from a Japanese *happi* coat (a traditional lightweight cotton jacket worn mostly during festivals).

Milligan's is a bold statement: padded and quilted with a huge, oversized hood. She has meticulously adorned it with an epic golden dragon, which is a foil screen-print of her own drawing. It has incredibly intricate hand-embroidered patches on the front, one of which has been turned into a pocket. They are surrounded by antique embroideries taken from a vintage kimono. 'The patches alone took me weeks to complete. The process is very slow, but I wouldn't have it any other way, everything I make has to be luxurious and all done by hand.' The jacket is finished off with neon pink hand-cut PVC flowers, Swarovski crystal beads and a special hand-embroidered label with the client's name stitched in the back.

Born and raised in rural Nottinghamshire, Milligan was keen to leave her village school and get to the city, where she studied her A levels and art foundation course at New College Nottingham. 'I was desperate to get into town where there was more going on. I'd spend my lunch breaks trawling the charity shops on Mansfield Road and haberdasheries in the Lace Market, finding things I could use in my work.' This is how she operates in Stroud now, networking with the local antique dealers to find beautiful textiles.

She had always longed to do her degree at Central Saint Martins in London and managed to secure a place on the prestigious fashion print course, having never made a garment before. During her second year, she made her first kimono for Grayson Perry. She worked closely with him throughout the project and created a baby pink quilted kimono adorned with embellished prints of hand-drawn retro toys and space guns. She was awarded second prize in her class, winning an original piece of his ceramic art. 'It was a joy to work with Grayson. He was an incredible tutor, who gave us honest and concise advice so we could create something he truly loved and wanted to wear.'

In the year that followed, Milligan interned in Paris, working for Christian Dior and Maison Lemarié, an atelier founded in 1880 which specialises in very high-end flower and feather work for the Parisian haute couture houses. She spent her days there choosing feathers and fabrics from their magnificently extensive storerooms, and then developed them into beautiful fabric samples for Chanel, one of which was chosen by Karl Lagerfeld to be made into a dress for the upcoming show. She loved working with the highly skilled older French artisans, learning traditional techniques of embellishment, and her experience in Paris reinforced her love for luxurious intricate handcrafted clothes.

For her final collection at Central Saint Martins, Milligan created a collection of oversized, quilted and highly adorned kimono hoodies. Sponsored by Swarovski, she hand stitched each one of them with iridescent crystals. She was one of the select few whose work made it to the press show, and this led to her entire graduate collection being hired by Christina Aguilera for her 'Liberation' comeback tour. After the tour she was asked if she would sell the kimonos to the superstar for her personal collection to be hung in her Hollywood home.

After graduating and then spending a few years working for brands in London, she needed time out from the city and moved to Stroud, thinking she'd only spend a few months in the countryside … it turned into three years! 'There's a calmness to Stroud I feel suits me better than London. Being surrounded by all these beautiful valleys, it's easy to escape and find tranquillity. I find there's a real collaborative spirit here where people want to help each other out and work together rather than being competitive. Of course it's easier being a fashion designer in London but I'm paving my path the slow and scenic route … plus my dogs love it!'

In 2019 Milligan was commissioned by the V&A Museum to make a piece for the 'Kimono: Kyoto to Catwalk' exhibition. It was then that she made her biggest, most epic kimono to date. Titled 'Fuji Heartbreak', the piece is enormous at nearly 3m in length, with a hand-painted fantasy landscape as the backdrop, where a mythical lion dog flies, cherub babies float on clouds and a geisha sits on a boat with two poodles. It's all linked together with haikus and song lyrics depicting the sorrows, hopes and optimism of enduring heartbreak.

The kimono took around six months to complete and truly was a labour of love. The sleeves and hood are literally dripping with old chandelier crystals, antique kimono prints turned into cartoon characters and old English embroidered napkins cut up and appliquéd to create the landscape. 'I feel like this kimono is less a fashion garment and more a piece of art, best hung in a gallery or on a wall. I think I prefer this way of working – spending a very long time on something and being able to tell a story at the same time.' The Stroud Valleys Artspace let her use their gallery space for a three-week residency while she finished the piece when it outgrew her flat. This was a great opportunity for the community to see a project come to life. She invited members of the public to come and help embroider the epic kimono as a way of passing on her skills to younger people and making the experience more fun and sociable.

Through the residency Milligan made lots of new connections, mainly with teenagers who are keen to go on to study textiles and fashion. She often has them assist her in the studio with current projects as well as supporting and guiding them with their school and college work.

Milligan also helps to run a young artist collective called 'Mould', which is supported by the SVA and has been running for many years. 'It's a way of getting young people together to produce work and put on shows without the constraints and structures of the education system. They get to decide what they want to do without boundaries. It's super chilled and we have a lot of fun.' Mould meet-ups are held twice weekly at the SVA and inclusive for anyone aged 15–20.

The future looks bright for Milligan Beaumont. She tells me that she's been offered a highly competitive grant from the Arts Council, and she will spend the next six months developing her creative practice. 'I've always felt somewhere in between fashion, art and textiles, and I create garments that sometimes would look better on a wall than a body. This grant will give me the opportunity to delve more into fine art and push my practice further, learning new skills in ceramics which I will combine into my kimono to create fantastical installations.'

Instagram: @milliganbeaumont

Noemi Gregoire
and Patrick Redfern
(Noi and Fish)

CLOTHES DESIGNER / DRUM MAKER AND DWELLING BUILDER

What comes across in conversation with Noi and Fish is their zest for their way of life, how well read they are, how passionate they are about their craft and how resilient they are. It would be fair to say they live a colourful, handmade life. 'We are all about food, clothes and shelter,' they say. And it's true, there is always a meal on the go when visiting them, always creativity going on.

Patrick (Fish) makes traditional bow-top caravans and shamanic drums; Noemi (Noi) is a textile artist. Together with their three children, the couple live in a quiet woodland in one of his handmade wagons with a small lean-to room built on to the side.

We sit around a roasting wood burner together, on sheepskin-covered benches, drinking coffee and eating toasted teacakes. The windows in the top of the wagon have Fish's own designs of etched glass. We overlook their vegetable patch and garden.

Noi

As a child, Noi was always making things. From the age of 12, she was using a sewing machine to make dolls clothes. 'Then I tried to make my own dress, but without knowing about pattern cutting it was tricky to get the fit right. Fairly quickly I learned more dressmaking skills, like cutting on the bias.

'When I was a teenager, I started to adapt things. If my trousers weren't baggy enough, I would sew darts of contrasting fabrics into the legs, and if they weren't long enough, I would unpick the hems and let them down, so they touched the ground. I found with clothing that nothing I bought fitted properly or looked quite right, so I had to change everything, taking things in and letting things out or adding bits. I used to wear the craziest things and would walk to college every morning feeling self-conscious, because I wanted to wear my own style but didn't want to be stared at. I had braided hair and would wear scarves around my head and huge earrings. Every day was a different outfit.

'I didn't study textiles at college, I was more drawn to fine art. I think because I was good at drawing, I just went with that. I was at Stroud College for three years and in the last year I started to question what I wanted to do. None of the university courses that touched on what I wanted to do covered everything. Either you did textiles, or you did fine art, or you did a craft, which was wood, metal and plastics but didn't involve textiles or fine art. I didn't want to study fashion because it didn't align with my values.'

Noi first had a stall at Stroud Farmers' Market when she was 14 years old. She sold dreamcatchers and bracelets with a couple of school friends. At 16, she started making macramé gem jewellery. When she was 18, she met Patrick (Fish) at the market.

'For my final project of the foundation course I made myself a mustard yellow nuno-felted dress. I was at Glastonbury Festival with Fish that year and people kept stopping me to ask where I had bought my dress. I went home and made six nuno-felted garments to take to Buddhafield Festival two weeks later. I sold them all and met my first regular customer, who went on to commission her wedding dress from me.

'When I was 19, I wanted to make myself a waistcoat, and I had a slightly felted old jumper, so I cut the sleeves off and made a collar and pockets from the sleeves. All the pieces left were like triangles, so I sewed them on to make fastenings and made toggle buttons from wood. Then I made one for Fish and one for my mum, then I made six and put them in Made in Stroud.

'We went to India and while we were there the waistcoats all sold. I remember going to the cashpoint in Pushkar and finding money in my account, which felt amazing.' When she returned, Noi bought lots of woollen garments from jumble sales and car boot sales, and started collecting materials to make more clothing in the yurt where they were living on a farm at the time. She used the same electric Singer sewing machine she'd had since she was 12 years old.

Noi currently makes two main lines of clothing: upcycled and felted. The inspiration for her clothing designs is a combination of aesthetic and practicality, teamed with her passion for the environment by reusing and making materials. Her kids' clothing range is based on providing cosy, warm, easy-to-wear clothing that lasts. Her womenswear is made using upcycled cashmere and wool, with occasional linen collections, and is designed to be flattering, cosy and unique. Her distinctive style translates into dresses, tops, jumpers and cardigans and her nuno hand-felting into exquisite dresses, tops and waistcoats. Considering she has three young children and lives 'off-grid' in the woods with no running water, she is impressively prolific, making whole collections every season and an increasingly adventurous line in brooches and 'pocket friends' (woodland animals from offcuts). She also makes hats, headbands, mitts, bags and a range of clothing for children. Noi recently made a pair of swans from French linen, one of which was snapped up by a collector in America.

Noi and Fish are also to be found in the Green Crafts field at Glastonbury, the Big Green Gathering and Shambala festivals every summer, teaching workshops, and they do a stall at Buddhafield. Noi teaches people to make felted waistcoats and dresses. She also makes wedding dresses and bridesmaid dresses to order, and her customers include TV presenters who have chosen her work to wear for media events.

Noi emphasises the importance of those customers who really believe in you and encourage you in your success, who go on to commission your work and are really supportive. She says they give a maker more

'You learn a lot from mistakes, and making a mistake can inspire you and can lead you on to something else.'

confidence. Noi gets several wedding dress commissions every year and loves making to order for special occasions.

Like many makers, Noi carries out her research by reading books and is constantly looking at ways to maintain her ethics around sustainability, using natural materials and upcycling while creating unique quality garments that people will love wearing many times over. The historical context of Stroud being the home of 'trade cloth' and the tradition of women being engaged in the textile arts are a hot topic with Noi. She is a great advocate of being self-taught, and says, 'You learn a lot from mistakes, and making a mistake can inspire you and lead you on to something else.'

Website: www.nimpyclothing.co.uk

Instagram: @nimpyclothing

Email: nimpyclothing@yahoo.co.uk

Fish (Patrick Redfern) – Drum Maker and Dwelling Builder

'My craft came out of a way of life, living on the earth, a kind of necessity of wanting to travel with the horse and wanting some kind of shelter. I make live-in structures which have a small footprint and don't make a massive scar on the environment – self-sufficient living.'

Fish began his journey into making when walking his horse Sam from a field he was living in in the Cotswolds to Wales, while living in a tipi. While he was in Wales, he built his first bowtop using a book, *The English Gypsy Caravan*, which he describes as 'the bible of wagon building'. The book didn't really have plans, it just had some scale drawings. Because of that, he made some mistakes – using the wrong wood. He used very heavy ash instead of pine.

The idea was to walk back with the horse and the wagon, but Fish's horse refused to pull the wagon because it was too heavy. So, he ended up walking back to Stroud with the horse and left the wagon, which was later transported by friends on a trailer. 'I based myself up near Sheepscombe in a shed in a field and started building more wagons. I sold the first wagon, and built another one to live in. There was a succession of selling a wagon and making another one and living in that. I sold wagons to writers, musicians, people who wanted a quiet place to sit out in the garden with a wood burning stove.'

> 'I make live-in structures which have a small footprint and don't make a massive scar on the environment – self-sufficient living'

Fish then started getting work for horse-drawn travellers doing repaints, recanvassing and repairs. The carved work on the wagons is quite intricate and is done by hand using a rounded rasp and a chisel. The roof beams are steamed and that's where the drum making came from. Fish was working on a yurt-making course, steam bending a hoop out of ash, and had the idea of offering drum-making workshops in the Green Fields at Glastonbury.

That was in 2003 and he's being doing this ever since. This is more about teaching practical skills than it is about selling drums. 'People today have a real yearning to learn a craft in a community setting. People come and share their problems and their successes with others over a three-day process, which culminates in having a henna-decorated drum with a handmade felt beater. An amazing instrument which they will keep forever. A sacred object. It's a journey. It's difficult in some parts, you have to go through the dark valley of the physical hard work and dealing with the deer skin, then you get to the plateau where the sun is shining and you finish your drum.'

Fish also makes onion bhajis every evening from the kitchen in his bowtop, which he tows to festivals. He is highly regarded for these snacks and for his secret spice mix.

Email: p_fish_mani@hotmail.com

Pascale Stanley

JEWELLERY DESIGNER

Pascale works from her loft studio in Victoria Works, a converted mill next to the canal in Chalford which houses a collective of local makers. She has furnished the space with uplifting pieces including some inherited from her Granny, with the aim of making the studio feel homely, and it certainly does. Her work table is a leather-topped vintage wooden desk and on this sits an old handmade set of engineer's drawers.

Pascale's love of geometrical statement tribal wear is evident in her designs and on her vision board. She has images and objects for inspiration on the walls above her workstation. Seahorses, ferns and ammonites are a theme, as are the moon cycles, astrology and the wheel of the year. Much of her design inspiration comes from nature and a north-African influence from family pieces belonging to her grandmother.

Pascale's studio workspace reflects her love of found objects and vintage, things that have a story and heritage, reflecting her fascination and intrigue with the connection between the object and its source, which are used widely in her design process. Her grandad settled in north Africa, where her mum was born and brought up, and he learned Arabic and developed a love of the culture. His love of all things north African led to him collecting tribal artefacts and treasures, and when Pascale was a child, he gave her an Agadez cross from the Tuareg Tribe – the four points of the traditional cross represent the four directions of the earth. The handcrafted silver amulet would have traditionally been passed from father to son as a family heirloom.

This piece proved to be very influential in her life, leading her to become more and more interested in the inspiration behind traditional design, and to eventually pursue a path in jewellery design. Pascale grew up playing with beautiful costume jewellery and wonderful dressing-up clothes and was inspired to develop a love of design and adornment, going on to make designs based on the concept of amulets and heirloom pieces.

Growing up with her mum working as a life model and maker, Pascale was inspired to be creative. She was always encouraged to play with new materials, often attending the after-school clubs and playgroup where her mum ran crafting activities.

After having graduated with a degree in arts and event management, Pascale lived in Bristol and spent some time working on various community projects and the festival scene. However, she become suddenly chronically ill. She was no longer able to work in events and had to take time out to recover.

While previously travelling in central and south America with friends, Pascale had met indigenous travelling artisans and had spent time with them, learning the traditional craft of wirework. As part of her healing process, she decided she needed to reconnect with her true calling and change direction. This led to an epiphany and a turning point in her life.

Pascale began to revisit and explore wirework and invested in some tools with the idea of perfecting the craft, not for any commercial gain, but as a therapeutic activity. After some time designing and making, she began sharing her designs with friends, who were very encouraging and bought her wirework earrings. Wanting to develop her work, she found a teacher and mentor in Kim Thomson, whom she cites as someone who's been a real inspiration and help to her throughout the years, making metal working more accessible and removing the mystery.

Pascale was fortunate to be accepted for an Enterprise Programme with the Prince's Trust and attended free courses on product photography along the way to help with her marketing. The Prince's Trust paired her with a mentor who had a corporate financial background and they helped her to think about the practical aspects of running her craft as a business, learning to see failure as a good thing – because if you don't fail you haven't tried – and encouraging her to approach galleries and learn to overcome fear of rejection, such a massive thing for all artists.

Having developed her range of 'Cheeky Danglers' spiral wire earrings, which she describes as a therapeutic practice, she has returned to doing more metalwork and traditional silversmithing techniques or, as she puts it, 'playing with fire'. 'My favourite part of the design process is trying a technique for the first time and getting amazing results! I love the pure play and experimentation, getting into a creative flow and feeling lost in time, seeing a design from my imagination or a sketch come to life and take on its own character.'

Environmental considerations have influenced her choices of materials while developing her style. She initially used a lot of brass but now there is more recycled silver and bronze. She's also now working with Fairmined or recycled gold in her wirework. She recycles all her scraps to be more earth friendly, uses recycled metals and likes to use stones from sustainable ethical sources.

Pascale has a collection of stones from her travels, which she treasures and occasionally makes into power pieces. Her collection includes a large azurite and malachite she brought back from South America. She has photographs of bespoke pieces she has made for family from her treasured collection of precious stones. For her parents' ruby wedding anniversary she made a ruby and zoisite pendant, set in gold fill, for her dad to give to her mum. The colours of this stone are quite incredible.

In her design work she uses reticulation, a heating process. Using a blowtorch, she melts alloys, balancing various intensities of heat and creating an organic texture on the finished piece. Because the two metals in an alloy, for example silver and copper in sterling silver, have different melting points, the technique creates an experimental surface and a unique piece of jewellery. Pascale describes the technique as 'unpredictable and deeply satisfying'. The resulting undulating texture can resemble mountains or sea, or can look like an ancient piece of jewellery found at a burial mound.

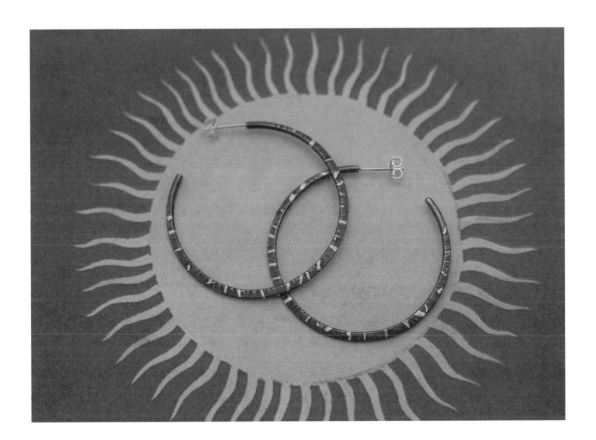

As part of her personal enquiry, Pascale has spent time working on a deeper level with the energy of the current moon cycle, while studying the traditional feminine energy and cycles in nature and astrology. She has been looking at working with the moon energies in a creative way in day-to-day life and relating to other people, focussing on making pendants which are talismans, with energy and intention going into the piece she is working on.

In doing so, her making process has shifted to be in tune with the moon cycle and astrology. So, she will make her moon pendants when the moon is in a certain sign, perhaps making a series of Taurus moons which take on the energy of that sign or allowing people to buy and wear jewellery which relates to the wearer's own astrology. This enquiry has inspired her Thirteen Moons collection and her feminine power pendants.

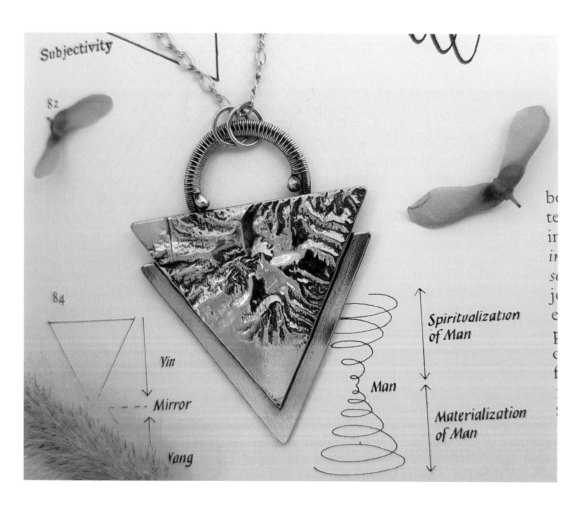

Pascale's feminine power pendants are made using the downward triangle symbol, which represents feminine power, the yoni, or sacred womb space, as well as the elements water and earth, both associated with the feminine signs in astrology such as Taurus, an earth sign, and Scorpio, a water sign. These power pendants are made with passion and are all about the wearer reclaiming their feminine power. They combine her fine detail of wirework with a big chunky piece of brass. Her favourite pieces have the unique reticulated surface with a very detailed wire-woven bail where the chain attaches, as the process is all about embodying the feminine and balancing the elements. 'The power pendant is a design I created at the beginning of last year, inspired by the incredible Tuareg jewellery passed on to me from my grandad. The Tuareg people of the Sahara Desert have a matrilineal society, meaning the blood lines are traced back through women rather than men. They hold very different traditions to most Muslim cultures in that the women are sexually free and they do not cover their faces in public; it is rather the men that do this! They also hold ownership of the family tent and animals. Their bold and beautiful jewellery is really reflective of this potent feminine power, and I wanted to recreate this in my own designs!'

Pascale is working on getting some pieces cast in recycled bronze or silver so that she has a more accessible range. She has also been looking at the seasonal energies of equinox, which would have been traditionally observed with ritual and ceremony in cultures from Celtic to Egyptian, equinox being all about the equal balance of dark and light. Through this study she has released the Equinox collection, designed around new beginnings.

This collection features the ancient Korean art of Keum-boo, which Pascale describes as a creatively brilliant process involving the application of delicate shapes and patterns of fine gold foil to silver. The silver is then blackened with an oxidation solution, creating a beautiful contrast and visually stunning piece of jewellery.

www.pascalestanley.co.uk

Instagram: @pascalestanley_jewellery
Facebook: pascalestanleyjewellery
Email: jewellery@pascalestanley.co.uk

Penny and John West

POTTERS

- *Lansdown Pottery* -

The three of us sit around a roaring wood burner in a converted barn, drinking coffee and eating home-baked cake while John and Penny tell me about their life together and how they came to run their own pottery. 'We met in 1983 when we were both living and working in Camphill communities. We have been married since 1993.'

John was originally involved in several arts and crafts and had moved to William Morris House in Eastington to become a weaver. However, as the community already had a weaver, it was suggested to John that if he had learned one craft, maybe he could learn another. The community had a potter who was leaving that summer and he could become her replacement.

With no experience in potting at all, John literally learned to make pots while teaching the craft. 'At the time, clay was this disgusting material in an allotment that I'd had in the New Forest!' he laughs. 'On a good day, I was on page eight and the students were on page five, and a bad day was when they were on page eleven and I was stuck on page nine! The first job I did was to spend about four hours smashing a room full of unfired pinch pots and putting them into dustbins I had found, putting water on them and turning them back into clay as there was no budget for new clay.'

John also went to evening classes at the Centre for Science and Art with Colin Gerrard when it was the Art College. Until recently, John and Penny had their teaching studio there. 'Learning to throw took a day or two,' he says. He had tuition from various potters who visited and stayed in the community, coming from the Grange in the Forest of Dean, Ruskin Mill and Cotswold Chine.

Penny was also originally a weaver, teaching at a Camphill community in Sussex and eventually moving to Eastington, where she took over the weavery at William Morris House. There she made hand-dyed mohair blankets, which were sold from a stall at Stroud Farmers' Market when it first started. In fact, they were at the very first farmers' market and sold their pots from day one in the Made in Stroud shop.

In the late eighties and early nineties, Penny and John created and ran training courses in crafts for Camphill co-workers, taking on apprentices for two years at a time.

Penny started potting in 2000, after the couple moved on from Camphill and took over the whole of the lower ground floor of the former art college, renamed the Centre for Science and Art. 'It was the best decision we ever made,' says Penny. 'We wanted to create a social

pottery where anyone could come and feel welcome. Whether they had learning difficulties, mental health issues or had always wanted to learn to pot. An outreach workshop on behalf of the William Morris community. We wanted to offer an integrated experience.' This was the beginning of Lansdown Pottery.

Because a lot of pottery courses were closing in schools and colleges at the time when they were setting up the studio, there was a lot of relatively cheap equipment available, meaning they were able to pick up affordable wheels. 'Part of our philosophy of working with people of all abilities is not to use "school clay", which is cheap, really forgiving and which we felt was disrespectful to the student, so we have always used a high-quality, expensive and strong clay to make a long-lasting item.'

In 2013 Penny and John bought some old farm buildings in Whiteshill to build a home and pottery. They live in a converted barn, the showroom is an old shepherd's cottage, and the studio is an old piggery with a sloping floor. Here they have a series of kilns, some manufactured, and some hand built in situ.

John sees pottery as an all-encompassing subject. He finds it fascinating when he's teaching people that they are excited by different aspects of the process. He cites the 3D element of throwing and building, the decorating, where the pot becomes the canvas, the chemistry, mixing the powders to create the glazes and the combination of all of these things – the pyromania, the love of sitting in front of a kiln watching the flames and throwing wood in. He is also interested in the geology of the art, using locally available materials. John has a collection of many of the rocks that exist on earth in a display case.

John transferred their holistic understanding of craft experience into a document for Ofsted called 'The Circle of Learning' to illustrate the value of the skills being used.

While building their own studio at their home, the couple took on a smaller space in the Centre for Science and Art, formerly the janitor's flat. Here, they had a series of rooms they used as a teaching studio, a throwing room, a hand-building studio, a glazing room, a damp room for pot storage and a library. There was an electric kiln for the initial firing and the students' work was glaze fired up at Whiteshill after bisque firing.

After twenty-two years at the centre, Penny and John finished teaching to concentrate on developing their own work. Alongside teaching, they have always made their own work for sale.

> 'We wanted to create a social pottery where anyone could come and feel welcome.'

Their current range of work falls into two main categories: their 'production pottery', tableware sold through shops and markets, and their 'studio pottery', sold privately and through exhibitions and shows.

Lansdown Pottery has four production glazes: Ocean Blue, Burnt Sienna, Bamboo and Ash Blue. They make stoneware which is unusually sturdy and oven/microwave/dishwasher proof. Their studio work, however, is more experimental and ornamental, using various techniques.

The firing of the wood kiln is started off with gas and then wood is added. There must be enough seasoned, dried, chopped and stacked wood to stoke the kiln all day and into the evening. Wood firing is slow, labour intensive and creates a unique effect, giving a strong, bright tone with incredible vibrancy. It requires constant attention and stoking and cannot be left.

This particular kiln was designed and built during the first summer at their new home by Joe Finch, who was originally from Winchcombe Pottery. It has two stoking holes, and the flame rises inside the arch of the kiln then goes down underneath the floor and back up the chimney.

Small refractory pads are attached to the bottom of each pot when loaded into the kiln to prevent it sticking to the shelf. These pots tend to be more expensive as there is so much more process involved in their production, either painting sodium bicarbonate on to the wood as a paste and introduced into the kiln that way, or wrapped up in newspaper parcels, dampened and introduced through the stoking hole, or as a spray, through the various openings in the kiln.

The rocket box, a much smaller kiln, is used for re-firing to perfect the final product.

The selling year usually begins with local Open Studios and the Select Art Trail, and the making for the season ideally begins in January. This is followed by a number of national pottery shows over the summer and autumn. The aim is always to begin making products for Christmas events in September after the summer shows, but John says it's often tricky getting in the mood to make Advent candle holders when the sun is blazing outside.

John's inspiration and fascination is with Japanese, Korean and Asian pots, and the whole aesthetic around the making, which is different from that in the West. 'There is almost a Zen approach, which is partly what makes it enjoyable. It's not just about making something, it's a personal journey.' He talks about an inner journey, not just an outer one, which he hopes the piece will emanate to the person who ends up owning the pot.

Pottery is becoming commonly recognised as a 'mindful' activity. 'It doesn't happen very often, but I have some wonderful times throwing pots. My wheel has a little tick to it as the wheel goes round. I remember one day where I had an amazing piece of music on which was in rhythm with the wheel and the pots were just perfect. At that moment, I looked out of the window and there were buzzards circling in the sky above the valley, and the world became one and I was just part of it. The whole activity of making a pot was part of the world rhythm. Each pot can become almost a mantra in that way.'

Penny puts it this way, 'Throwing is not something you can do while thinking about something else, or when not feeling OK. If you're in a bad mood, do something else. It is impossible to centre the clay unless you are centred in yourself.'

www.lansdownpottery.co.uk   www.johnwestatlansdown.co.uk

Instagram: @lansdownpottery
Facebook: lansdownpottery
Email: lansdownpottery@onetel.com

Rosie May Hofman

JEWELLERY DESIGNER

From her home studio in town, Rosie designs and makes timeless, ethical, unisex jewellery which infuses intricate yet bold minimal design. 'I make playful designs that mimic nature's geometry, in materials that elevate people and earth. My creations can be strung, stacked and interconnected in striking combinations, with tactile, movable components. My work is genderless and invites the wearer to create their own narrative.'

Rosie's dog Luna lies in the sun while she works. Her dad has made her a beautiful jeweller's workbench in slate grey. A vision board of inspiration and ideas fills the wall of her bright and tidy studio. She explains she has a fascination for the naturally occurring patterns in nature, from space all the way to the earth, into micropatterns in nature, macro patterns on a cellular level and the correlation between shapes and forms.

Rosie May Hofman was brought up in the Stroud valleys and grew up around two very creative and practical parents. As a child she was always intrigued by taking things apart, and would watch her dad who, in addition to doing maths and physics at Cambridge University, was a shoemaker, carpenter and fixer of everything, and renovated the family home. Rosie's mum is very creative and did lots of print making along with being an art teacher and healer.

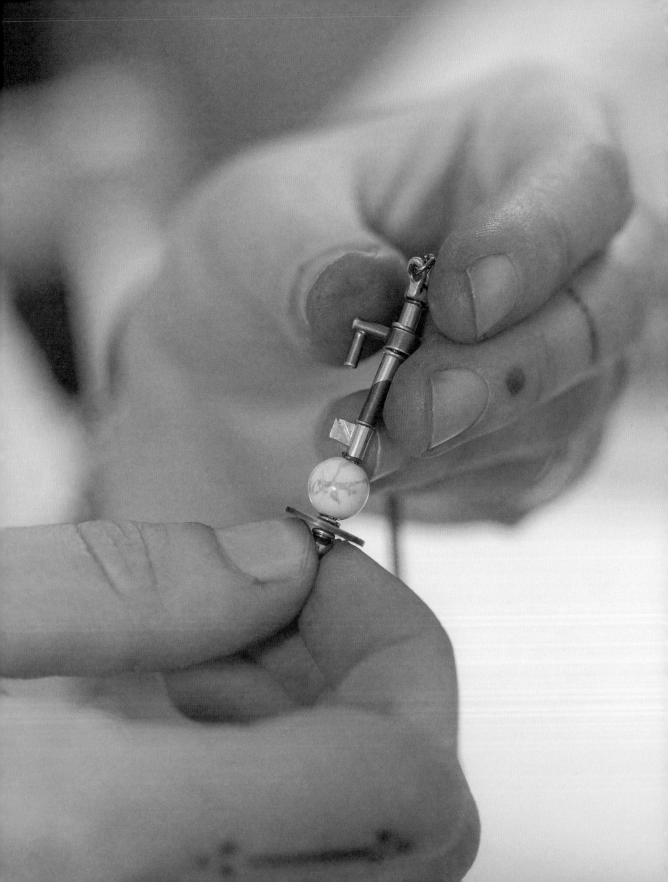

Rosie found that the education system really didn't suit her and she found school difficult as she is dyslexic, but always shone in the arts and textiles and was always at the top of her class in those subjects. Rosie started making and selling jewellery from the age of 13, something her parents really encouraged, and she would set up a little table to sell in the street.

Rosie was thinking of doing an art foundation course but found out she could do silversmithing and jewellery design as a degree so decided instead to apply to Birmingham School of Jewellery, where she was accepted without a foundation in art, which is quite unusual. 'I've just always been one of those people who know that was my calling and I also come from a family where everyone is self-employed, so it came very naturally to me to set up my own business.'

Once Rosie got to uni, it became clear to her that, to stand out, she needed to develop a strong style and this was what she really put her efforts into trying to discover. She did a HND in jewellery design and silver smithing, combining traditional and modern techniques like laser welding. The final year was in 3D design and included the use of CAD (computer-aided design) and product design to help with problem-solving designs and working out the most efficient way to make pieces so they are affordable, rather than using traditional design methods.

While she was at uni and developing her designs, she wanted to define her influences and her style. Her mum suggested that they get out all Rosie's previous projects and sketchbooks and draw out the common themes, which Rosie feels was a powerful process from which she honed her style from a very personal and instinctive place which she finds hard to articulate. In her final year, she developed her signature 'Talis' necklaces with moving components, which are still part of her range and represent her 'strong style'.

'I'm really passionate about our innate need as humans to adorn and express ourselves and I've also taken up tattooing. I'm fascinated by the way that jewellery, unlike clothing, outlives us.' Rosie loves the fantasy that our jewellery will tell stories in the future about what our culture was like and what individuals of our time were like, leading her to work in an environmental and ethical way, 'so that there is someone to discover my work in the future and wonder about it'.

As a reflection of her personal values, Rosie is a Fairmined registered maker, meaning that all gold plating and most commissions use gold from artisan miners and the money goes back into building their local communities. Fairmined transforms mining into an active force for good, contributing to institutional, social and environmentally sustainable development. Through the Fairmined standard, they promote responsible mining, helping miners to improve their practices and generate change in their communities, and facilitate access to fair markets. While recycled metal is great, Rosie feels it completely ignores the needs of

'My creations can be strung, stacked and interconnected in striking combinations, with tactile, movable components.'

the artisanal and small-scale mining sector, which employs approximately 42 million people with more than 150 million people worldwide depending on this activity to make a living.

Rosie moved to Bristol, worked hard on trying to find her feet and trying to set up a business, and for about three years developed her geometrical collection which are now her bestsellers. She built the brand organically, working part time for other jewellers. She worked for Rachel Entwistle in London, travelling up every weekend to work in the shop on Saturdays and Sundays and then moving to London and working for her.

She ended up doing an internship with Polly Wales before Polly relocated to California. During this time, she says she learned so much from working with a trailblazer and such a successful person and very much enjoyed the experience and inspiration. 'I learned some awesome techniques and was helping with casting and I found it inspiring how Polly was a mum, working from home, and was such a trailblazer. It was amazing to be around that kind of person. There was a moment where I thought I could either work for someone amazing or I could follow my dream, and I decided to follow my dream to set up my own brand.'

Around this time, Rosie came up with the triangle and circle pieces for her XY Collection, then suffered with anxiety and depression as she found living in London tough. She didn't enjoy how commercial work, which she found dull, was selling well: 'I ended up losing my way in the city life, that culture where being different wasn't celebrated, and where I felt bland design was favoured over bold design.'

In 2017 she moved back to Stroud, where she describes finding herself again, feeling it was OK to be her authentic self and following her own design direction, to have her own unique style. Since returning to Stroud, she feels she has gone from strength to strength. Originally renting a studio in Thrupp, she eventually moved back home, where she is working towards building a studio in the back garden.

Rosie gave up her last part-time job in 2018 to focus on her jewellery making and tattooing. She loves having the second creative outlet of body art and really enjoys the way her tattoos look with her jewellery. 'My work comes from a tapestry of influences, and I love the fact that my work is quite abstract as it invites the viewer to create their own interpretation. Instead of naming things in an obvious way, I don't, I allow it to be ambiguous.

Rosie is inspired by action and loves her work to contribute to solutions by donating to organisations and creating awareness, as well as planting a tree for every sale.

Rosie's day always begins with taking Luna for a long walk in the nearby valleys before deciding if it's an admin day or a making day, depending on how she feels in the morning. Obviously, orders come first, but she loves the flexibility of self-employment. She regularly practises yoga for well-being and enjoys the local landscape.

Orders and commissions mainly come from markets, Instagram and existing customers. Rosie is a regular at Frome Independent Market, Bath Market, Stroud Farmers' Market and Bristol Harbourside and has built a loyal customer base and a strong mailing list through events. She sends out regular newsletters to her returning customers and finds Instagram good for her brand. She has seven stockists in the UK, including the Made in Stroud shop.

www.mayhofman.com

Instagram: @mayhofman
Email: info@mayhofman.com

Stephanie Cole

ILLUSTRATOR

Stephanie describes her work as predominantly in illustration, ranging from massive murals to her own range of greetings cards, stationery and client work. 'I'd describe my illustration as being inspired by the everyday, whimsical, simple and telling a story, while having a bit of a Scandinavian influence too.'

Stephanie was very art-driven growing up and her parents encouraged creativity at home. She says she was determined from a young age to follow her passion and in college completed a BTEC in art. Despite this, her parents were still worried that she didn't have anything to fall back on, but she was adamant that she would like a career in creativity.

After her BTEC in Cirencester, she studied art foundation in Cheltenham at the University of Gloucestershire. Her major at foundation level was in textiles, and as she wasn't clear whether she would like to do textiles or illustration, she decided to do a degree in surface pattern design in Swansea, giving her options for either as a career path. Her time there exploring different mediums and living by the sea she describes as 'wholesome and inspiring'.

After she graduated in 2010, she worked in retail for a short spell and couldn't see how she could make it back into a career in the arts. 'Seeing my predicament, my mum asked if I'd like to use the dining room to create. We set about moving the furniture out. I bought a print table from a charity shop and that became my studio. I was entirely grateful she gave me the opportunity and believed I could make it happen.' Steph began printing her own designs onto tote bags, cushions and tea towels, which she sold at events and through the Made in Stroud shop. While doing this, she got a part-time job for amazing fabric printing business Rapture and Wright, near Stow-on-the-Wold.

Steph was unsure whether to follow her own design passions or to make what she thought people would want for their Cotswold homes, starting off, she says, 'a bit tweedy'. She eventually found the courage to develop her own style and work in a way that she loved rather than doing what she thought was expected. This really paid off for her, and her work became popular.

The big breakthrough came when she moved to Finland in 2012 for two years with her partner, who is an animator. Moving to Scandinavia for Jordan's work was a spur of the moment decision, and the two had never lived together before. She left some stock with her mum, who managed her deliveries to shops and galleries for her.

She really enjoyed the creative freedom of being able to do whatever she wanted and moving away from the work she had been doing. Not having the facilities to print, and not being able to find work in Finland, she embarked upon a twenty-day drawing challenge for herself and posted it daily on social media. 'Having set myself the challenge and created my own accountability by posting daily on social media, I felt I would be letting people down (and myself) if I didn't post anything, so worked really hard at it. It was a brilliant and intense experience, and some of those designs are still among my best sellers.' Her illustration business took off from there.

Stephanie's work in the Made in Stroud shop was spotted by Westmorland buyers who were scouting for the newly built Gloucester Services while she was in Finland, and they commissioned her to paint murals on the walls in the farm shop, deli, butchers counter, play area and corridors to illustrate the values of the business. She had never done anything this scale before and, although nervous, threw herself into the work and was delighted with the reaction to her designs.

She was flown from Finland to the UK to hand paint the murals in the new buildings, which Steph describes as the 'dream job' from which most of her further work has come. Her mural work can now be seen in hotels in London, ice-cream parlours in Cornwall, Hobbs House in Nailsworth, schools, hospitals and homes nationally.

In 2018 Stephanie and Jordan got married at Berry Farm in South Cerney, arranging her whole wedding as a 'dream skill swap'. She updated the farm's branding and painted the venue's lovely barn conversion in return for the venue hire and wonderful platters of local produce to feed to guests. She bought her dream wedding dress by a Finnish designer second-hand online and made herself an embroidered and embellished denim jacket for the evening, hand stitched with daisies and the words 'Burning Love' emblazoned across the back (the Elvis song of the same name was the couple's first dance). She also skill-swapped branding work and painting for Hetty's Kitchen 'Cake Hatch' in Gloucester who, in return, created an incredible dessert bar and wedding cakes for the big day.

The couple travelled more with Jordan's work, first to Farnham, where Steph did some work for the craft town, and then spending four years living in Manchester where her son was born in 2019. The family have now moved back to Stroud. 'I've always considered Stroud my "spirit town". As a teenager, my parents used to take me to visit open studios in town and to the fashion events in Painswick. I always thought Stroud was bonkers and wonderful, so I'm delighted to be living here.'

Her work currently involves client illustrations and commissions for the Museum of Somerset and Port Sunlight village, a great example of how varied her work has become. In an effort to make her work more planet friendly, Stephanie has been spending time on reducing her packaging, doing away with cellophane packing for her greetings cards and replacing them with peel-off paper closures. To allow time for client work, her product range has been simplified to stationery, cards and art prints, the latter being printed to demand, to be more eco-friendly, and offering a much more immediate way for her to 'test the waters' with new work.

Stephanie now works increasingly digitally, meaning she can pick up her device and work in the evenings and at nap time without needing a studio. This enables her to carve out creative time while being a mummy. She previously used gouache and watercolours on paper and says that while digital can never replace that, it's a great immediate medium for the moment. She is enjoying working with seasonal flower images and looking at updating her range. She is also delving back into mural work for businesses and private homes to commission.Stephanie's work can be found on Not on The High Street, Etsy and select galleries and shops.

> 'I'd describe my illustration as being inspired by the everyday, whimsical, simple and telling a story, whilst having a bit of a Scandinavian influence too.'

www.stephaniecole.co.uk

Email: stephaniecole@live.co.uk

Susie Hetherington

DESIGNER

Coming from a background of graphic design, Susie describes her style as 'maximalist'. Her range of fabrics, soft furnishings and stationery have a gorgeously abundant feel. 'My process is all about detail, pattern and form first. Although I love colour, that very much comes later. Unless I'm doing some drawings just for fun, I tend to work in black and white.'

Describing her styles as 'nature inspired', Susie says, 'I always feel I'm only observing. The patterns are already out there and I am just repeating them.' Everything is drawn from within a few miles' radius of the house, her fabrics being named after places in the area. 'My mum always said when I was a toddler I took forever walking everywhere as I wanted to look at every stone and every leaf and I don't think that ever changed.'

Susie has always had a love of drawing and making things and was encouraged at primary school and at home to explore her creativity as she grew up. She also chose to be different from her very academic older sister and focus more on her creative side. Her mum was one of her teachers at school, where she was surrounded by encouraging adults, even having a kiln to use as part of the art syllabus, which she says wouldn't happen in primary schools now.

At secondary school she got into doing lots of drawing, painting and sculpture, going on to do art foundation at Falmouth College in Cornwall and exploring lots of disciplines. In the last term, Susie decided to focus on graphic design, something that was completely new to her, the appeal being it was quite ideas based. She stayed to do her degree in graphic design in Falmouth, which she describes as the most amazing place to go to university, and a place where she made lifelong friendships. 'At some point I became quite tight and controlled in my art and tried to unlearn that a bit at uni.'

Susie chose a career in graphic design, working for various agencies and a broad range of clients, becoming a specialist in brand identity. The commercial side of this work gave her a whole host of skills that she would come to use later.

In her mid-twenties, Susie became a founder of a branding consultancy near Bath, which went on to be successful. Wanting to concentrate on being a mum, she decided to let go of that work when she had her second daughter, selling her shares in the company and spending much more time at home, near Stroud.

With two young children who were close in age, the only way to get them to have a nap at the same time would be to go for a drive. With her babies sound asleep, she would park up on the common or in a car park and use the time to draw in sketchbooks.

Originally drawing for sanity, this turned out to be the thing that put Susie on the path to a new career. A friend showed her an article about Cameron Short, a printmaker in Dorset, who had worked in the advertising industry in London and had decided to change his life completely, moving to the country and doing an apprenticeship with the printmaker Marthe Armitage. Cameron had written a letter to Marthe and managed to get a scholarship from the QEST fund to support his apprenticeship.

Susie was really inspired by his work and managed to contact him to see if history would repeat itself. He phoned her back and was really supportive, telling her to get carving lino from home. While in Dorset with the family, Susie arranged to visit him, and he encouraged her in her dream.

Susie's third child was born in 2015. Already having a small range of products, she would still use the baby's nap times as a time for creativity and drawing: even lino cutting in the car if the baby had fallen asleep. Now, with all three children at school, she finds self-employment flexible for family life and says having limited time makes her more productive and decisive. She works most evenings and enjoys not having to travel to and from a studio for the time being.

Susie describes her typical day as walking the kids to school, then walking the dog on the way home, then working until school pick-up time. Her home studio is next to the kitchen and serves as storage for her work as well as a creative space. Her partner has made her a large cutting table and she has a plan chest full of lino blacks and a dresser full of cards, sketchbooks, cushions, fabrics, lampshades, packaging materials, lampshade-making kits, props for photo shoots, reference books, boxes of stock and endless lino blocks which she has hand carved.

Originally lino printing her work onto fabric, Susie now prints to paper and scans these and other drawings, to be reproduced digitally, so she can easily print by the metre.

She has found that her lino blocks are popular with visitors at Open Studios and describes them as old friends she could never part with. 'The blocks become objects in their own right and remind me of a time of awakening,' she says, enthusiastically.

Being from a background of graphic design, Susie already has Photoshop skills, which most artists must learn later. Describing her design process, she explains that she sometimes goes on a walk and sees two things that she draws, and they will end up both being in the same pattern. Sometimes, a fabric is one flower put together with a stripe. Drawing is purely for creativity, and the pattern always emerges later, before becoming a product. Susie says one of her challenges is to have a compact range of designs as products, as she would happily go on designing new patterns forever.

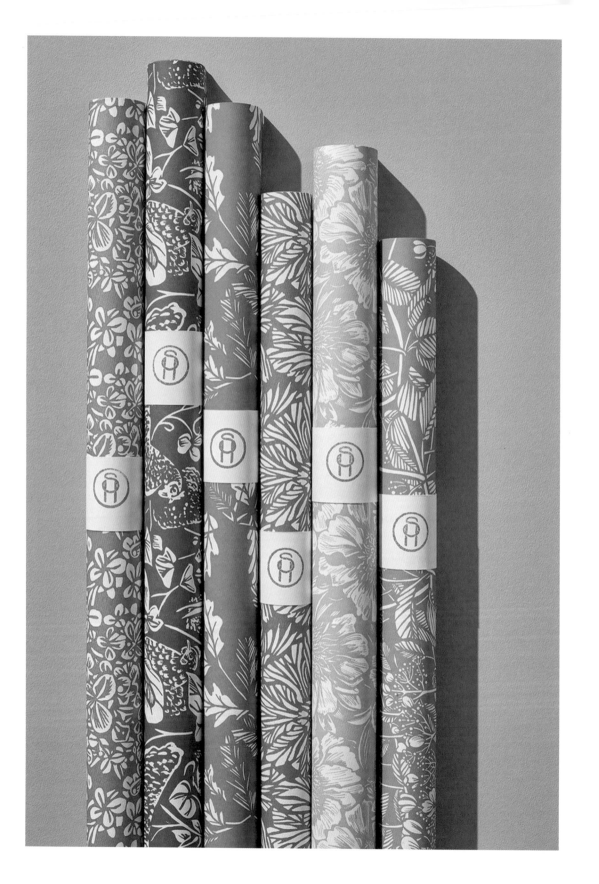

The selling is massively out of her comfort zone and is not something she enjoys at all. In the graphic design business that she owned, she was the creative lead, and her partners did most of the business side, which, she says, is definitely her preference.

Susie has three strands to her work: her design work, which goes into her textiles, wrapping paper and cards; her work as the creative lead for Three Storeys in Nailsworth; and her work with clients for branding and graphic design, such as her friend Fiona's company, Soap Folk (see page 73).

Describing her process, Susie says, 'I love doing the original drawing at the beginning but the bit that really really gets me is the bit after that, when I first put the pattern in repeat. I love carving; I find it very therapeutic and can lose myself in it. But the first time I print a repeat on paper, it becomes a curtain or a tablecloth in my own mind. Once the design is out there, I am almost over it and want to start again. It's all about the creative process for me.' She also loves showing her work and finds Instagram a great tool for this, finding her audience really encouraging and supportive.

Another joy of the design process is receiving photographs from customers and interior designers of her soft furnishings in homes, a whole other creative stage which can be so well executed. 'I received a picture of a blind a customer had had made in a custom colour and it worked very well in the room and made total sense with the garden beyond the window.'

Susie loves other people's creativity, like seeing on Instagram how people use her tea towels to make their own bunting or cushions and even patchwork, loving that the work has a life beyond her.

'I feel really lucky to work with my friends, Nicki, from Three Storeys and Fiona, from Soap Folk; they are gifts of clients. It's a joy to work with people from the beginning of a project, working on establishing a style together and adding new designs in an organic and natural way, as well as making decisions based on our values. It's such a contrast to working with big corporations whose values you don't share, which I have done a lot of in the past. For smaller companies, your work matters so much more.'

Susie loves working locally and one of the benefits for her are the repeat local customers, who can even be friends at the school gates. She loves working with small ethical businesses and being within walking distance of their HQs. 'I can no longer imagine how I travelled to London regularly for work, in the past. Now that would be an occasional treat, but for the most part I feel very rooted here.'

Susie's work can be bought from Made in Stroud and her own website.

www.susiehetherington.co.uk

Instagram: @susiehetheringtontextiles
Facebook: susiehetheringtontextiles
Email: susie@susiehetherington.co.uk

Victoria Sangwine-Gould

TEXTILE MAKER

~ Studio Vee ~

Victoria's textiles brand is based on sustainable and ethical business practices using reclaimed and upcycled fabrics to make beautiful and useful items that don't have a negative impact on the environment. Although she loves making, she says, 'I don't want to add to the world unnecessarily'.

Having always loved fashion and clothes, Victoria did an art foundation after doing art A level and then chose to do a degree in 3D design as she hated the toxic culture of fashion, both in terms of waste and in the competitiveness. She did a three-year degree at Ravensbourne in furniture and related product design.

She then got a job in a factory in Bury in Lancashire. 'Moving to Lancashire from Surrey was a massive culture shock and people thought I was a bit posh, although they were warm and welcoming. One of the girls in the office took me under her wing and let me sleep on her floor for three weeks while I found a house to rent.'

In the factory she would often work from 7.30 a.m., when it opened, and would stay on until 6 p.m., when everyone had gone home and there was some peace and quiet for getting on with designing. Victoria worked as a designer of sofas and chairs which were sold to mass-market shops like DFS and John Lewis. Her design ideas would come from visiting the foreign shows and seeing what was cool in Italy at the time.

Inspiration would come from surprising places, like seeing a curved chest of drawers at a show and interpreting that into a sofa design. Often the design brief would be based on price, rather than form, because of the mass-market nature of the work. She was also responsible for choosing fabrics and leather for upholstering the furniture. She is fascinated by people's perception of colours, and our general hesitancy to use bold colours in our homes, saying, 'I always think it would be really interesting to put on someone else's eyes'.

Victoria moved to Stroud in 2009, after her sister Gemma and another friend who live here arranged a blind date with Tony, and they got on well, eventually getting married. Like many skilled professionals moving here, it was obvious to Victoria that continuing with her previous career would not be an option locally due to the lack of industry in the area. She decided to go freelance, making her own products, and arranged to view a studio together with a friend, Nick, and Gemma. The three of them decided immediately to take on the lease, initially renting the top floor of the studio and later the whole place.

Although she does not make other people's curtains because of lack of space in the studio, she has really enjoyed making curtains and cushions for her own home, which is an old building with flagstone floors. Her home style is eclectic, with mostly antique furniture and modern sofas, and the couple do not shy away from colour – their hallway is Chinese yellow. They enjoy redecorating, with Victoria being a little more adventurous, and share a love of the same style. Victoria is a lover of home décor and a beautiful home environment.

Being freelance really suits Victoria, in terms of working hours and freedom of design. Not being a morning person, she will walk into the studio for around 10 a.m. to midday, then work until 7, when she is more productive. With her husband working away a lot, the flexibility of working freelance is appealing, meaning that when he is home, they can spend time together.

Since going freelance, Victoria has built on skills she already had. She has always been a competent sewer, but has become a better sewer and more accurate. She has learned more techniques and has become pretty competent with an industrial sewing machine.

Victoria has had to learn to market herself, which she still finds really challenging. She says she has learned a lot about herself and her strengths. 'Because I'm not a very good salesperson, my reputation has to come through the quality of my work. I take pride in making and finishing things well. If I make a mistake and I have to spend ten minutes unpicking and remaking something, I will. I want that to be my selling point. I don't like to big myself up as it doesn't feel from my heart, so I like my work to do the talking.'

Over this time, she has learned to make her product range reflect her personality, using fabrics like velvets, tweeds, menswear and suiting, which she feels have some 'guts', and materials that are not found in most shops, while sticking with the recycling theme and contemporary design. 'When I moved here, I felt a lot of pressure to make soft furnishings to fit in the cute Cotswold style, but I soon allowed myself to work with fabrics and designs that I love and to follow my own style.'

One of the first things which was quite important to Victoria when she started working for herself was to work with people she likes, whom she trusts and are prompt with payments, cutting out any stress and creating a good feeling around her working life. 'My favourite feeling is completing the first batch of a new product line and sending them out into the world. This was always my favourite job as a furniture designer, seeing hundreds of sofas coming off the production line after designing them.'

In the studio she has her trusty sewing machines, an industrial Brother and a Juki for sewing leather, plus her overlocker, the main tools for her trade. Radio 4 is on in the background constantly, and the walls are lined with rolls of fabric, crates and shelves of sorted, folded fabrics waiting to be made into accessories for home and fashion. There is always a cup of tea on the go.

Victoria's love of classic cars has led to an interest in learning reupholstering techniques, known as 'trimming'. She is working on a range of products that combine the aesthetic of car interiors in accessories. 'It's a cool look, the stitching and pleats, and there are some really interesting techniques involved', she says, and has been teaching herself for some time, having

been commissioned by a friend to do some work on his Volkswagen Sirocco. She is planning to re-cover the seats in her Lancia for fun.

As well as a 1981 red Lancia Beta Spider, Victoria has a 1988 Porsche 944 and a 1964 Triumph Herald. 'If I won the lottery tomorrow, I would go out and buy loads more and a get place to store them all!' She has worked for a classic car trimmer and learned quite a few techniques from him. He has been a car trimmer for thirty years and watching how he handled the materials was an eye opener. 'Using vinyl and leather is so different from using fabric. You have to be very precise and there is no room for error, because unpicking is not possible as you'd be left with holes in it. You have to be very precise. What I've found interesting is that because trimming is mostly male dominated, the charge is higher than for female-dominated crafts. Although the skills

are very similar to a dressmaker's, a trimmer's hourly rate is a lot more. When I was a furniture designer, I always knew in the back of my head that I wasn't earning as much a guy would be earning. I had the interiors of one of my cars redone, and the quality of the work is fantastic. When I worked back the hourly rate, I thought, "Yes, that's a proper wage." It's a masculine thing where maybe they are more confident to ask for more money.'

Victoria's trade clients are boutiques and interior designers based in the Cotswolds. Most of her private clients are people who find her by word of mouth or through social media. One of her clients, Alice from Humphries & Begg, works with textiles manufacturers and artisans in India to get her own designs printed onto cotton and linen, and Victoria makes up her piped cushions and soft furnishings for her using her own unique and very colourful fabric designs. She also makes work for Polly Lyster, a very successful local indigo dyer, selling through Egg in London, and Amy Perry Antiques, who buys her own antique fabric and linen collections in France which she gives to Victoria to make up into collections of soft furnishings.

Victoria has a natural love for art deco in interiors and seventies design, and finds she has got more appreciation of good design from lots of eras as she has got older. 'The power of nostalgia is something which changes our perception of what is cool,' she observes.

www.studiovee.co.uk

Instagram: @studioveestroud
Email: victoria@studiovee.co.uk

Illustration Credits

Lucy Mabley: carving lino, p. 12

Katie Jane Watson Photography: p.17

Lucy Harris: Bridget in her studio, p. 33

Henry Arden: family of jugs, p. 34

James Milroy: Bridget drawing through slip on a leather-hard plate, p. 36 (left)

Artist's own: a basket of pots fresh from the kiln, p. 36 (right); stack of pots, p.39

Bryony Milroy: retrogrey vases, p. 37

Dave Cockcroft with an eight-stick, high-back chair at its new home near Bala, Wales, p. 47; six high-back Welsh stick chairs in elm and oak, p. 49; eight high-back Welsh stick chairs in elm and oak, p. 50; eight high-back stick chairs ebonised for a traditional black finish, p.51; hand-carved wooden spoons, some have been ebonised, p. 52

Steve Russell Studios: pp. 61 & 64

Emily Lawlor: in garden studio, p. 60; vintage china mosaic bluetits, p. 62

Steve Russell Studios: vintage china mosaic swallows, p. 61; gold and white mosaic swans; p. 64

Karen Lawrence: Emmie working on a gown for a gala ball, p. 67

Emily McNair: jacket in emerald-green, bamboo silk, p. 68

Luke Coleman: Emmie sketches at the designing table, p. 69; vintage sewing tools on herringbone Harris tweed cloth, p. 70 (top)

The History Press

The destination for history
www.thehistorypress.co.uk